MW01164865

NFT (Non-Fungible Token):

The Easy Investing Guide for Beginners to Create, Buy, Sell, Trade, and Make Profit With Digital Crypto Art and Collectables

William Rick DeVito

© **Copyright 2021 - All rights reserved.**

The content contained within this book may not be reproduced, duplicated or transmitted without direct written permission from the author or the publisher.

Under no circumstances will any blame or legal responsibility be held against the publisher, or author, for any damages, reparation, or monetary loss due to the information contained within this book, either directly or indirectly.

Legal Notice:

This book is copyright protected. It is only for personal use. You cannot amend, distribute, sell, use, quote or paraphrase any part, or the content within this book, without the consent of the author or publisher.

Disclaimer Notice:

Please note the information contained within this document is for educational and entertainment purposes only. All effort has been executed to present accurate, up to date, reliable, complete information. No warranties of any kind are declared or implied. Readers acknowledge that the author is not engaged in the rendering of legal, financial, medical or professional advice. The content within this book has been derived from various sources. Please consult a licensed professional before attempting any techniques outlined in this book.

By reading this document, the reader agrees that under no circumstances is the author responsible for any losses, direct or indirect, that are incurred as a result of the use of the information contained within this document, including, but not limited to, errors, omissions, or inaccuracies.

Table of Contents

Introduction

NFTs (non-fungible tokens) are trending and will continue to do so for a while. It's not just being talked about in cryptocurrency circles but also on the news, social media pages, and more!

It's a buzzword that has gotten everyone curious to know what it is and how it all works. But most importantly, how they can benefit from using it.

NFTs are a concept that can be confusing at first and to most, especially those who don't know much about cryptocurrency. But once you have grasped it, your mind will be blown by just how amazing an opportunity this is and how important it is to be part of it.

Crypto art is a decade-old concept that was only privy to those early cryptocurrency adopters and investors. It was akin to inside information, to be shared and celebrated with like-minded individuals looking for cryptocurrency to change the world.

But all that is changing.

Since the cryptocurrency boom, with Bitcoin at the head and showing no sign of falling anytime soon, the technology has expanded, with NFTs taking center stage.

The COVID-19 pandemic helped with this; as many people around the world couldn't leave their homes, they found themselves with extra money to spend, and spend they did: online. Technology was what the global population turned to for entertainment and to find solace in a time of uncertainty.

With so many people online, various cryptocurrency businesses sprung up based around NFTs, with more on the way. Over $250 million worth of NFTs were traded in 2020, an increase of 299% from the previous year with this number set to rise even further (Iredale, 2021). Everyone is getting on board to be part of it, from celebrities to local artists to anyone looking to make some money by trading.

This is where you come in and why it's important to learn everything about NFTs and start on your trading journey. This is a beginner's guide, but will also be useful for those experienced in cryptocurrency and looking to break into this new and exciting venture.

It's important to note that I am not a financial advisor and am not registered to give out any financial advice. This is merely a guide based on information gathered. My book covers the basics of cryptocurrency and Bitcoin so that you have everything you need to understand how it all works, regardless of how much you already know. The basics of cryptocurrency are important, as well as the concepts that will be reiterated throughout the book.

If you already know everything about cryptocurrency and just want to figure out NFTs, then I have you covered as well. Just use the detailed Table of Contents to skip ahead to find the information you are specifically looking for.

Among other topics, I dive into what NFTs are in detail, including some interesting examples. These will give you an idea of what you are getting yourself into and why. And finally, I discuss how you can create your own NFTs and how to buy and sell these to make a generous passive income.

I have also included the risks and how to stay secure so that you don't go in blind.

It might seem mind-boggling at first, but I promise you the information sticks and will help you grasp NFTs with ease.

Now is the time to learn more and be part of history while also earning in the process!

Chapter 1:

Cryptocurrency

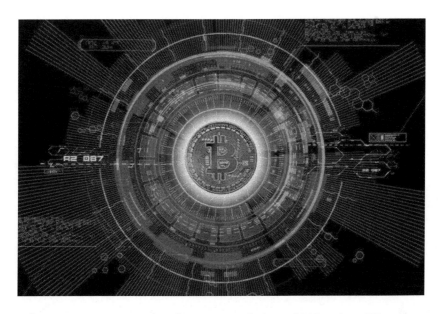

Modern cryptocurrency has been around since 2009, when Bitcoin was first released to the public. Now, in 2021, there are far more cryptocurrencies available, not just Bitcoin. The world of cryptocurrency is bigger than ever with various marketplaces for people to use around the world and new countries joining all the time.

Cryptocurrency has proven that it's not just for technology buffs or those wanting to change how the financial system works, but anyone can be and should be a part of it. Cryptocurrency is here to stay, and with it more advancements in technology, the latest being NFTs.

To truly understand NFTs, you need to know its background and that background starts with cryptocurrency's history.

The History of Cryptocurrency

Most cryptocurrencies today are variations of Bitcoin, which was the first widely used cryptocurrency. It was founded in 2009 by a programmer called Satoshi Nakamoto to bring in a new technological age of blockchain and decentralized digital currencies.

That sounds like a mouthful, but it will be made clear soon.

Satoshi Nakamoto is an anonymous name, as it is still unknown who they are or if they even exist at all. It is rumored that Satoshi Nakamoto is the pseudonym used by the creators of Bitcoin, so it is very possible that Satoshi Nakamoto could be a group of individuals instead of one person. If they were just one person they would be a billionaire now.

Bitcoin began with a whitepaper, which is a document that contains concise information about the subject it concerns. The Bitcoin whitepaper was released in 2008 and was revolutionary.

Bitcoin was the first cryptocurrency that is widely recognized today, but others predate it and had a hand in inspiring its creation.

Smart Cards

One of the first attempts made was in The Netherlands in the 1980s, with the creation of smart cards for gas stations that were prone to nighttime thefts. This was a huge problem because gas stations had to open overnight so that trucks could refuel. A bunch of developers got together and linked money to smart cards for the drivers to use. Truck drivers used the cards to pay, so that the gas stations kept no cash and couldn't be robbed.

Flooz

Flooze.com started using its e-currency in 1998, which was part of its marketing scheme. You could buy one Flooz for $1 and then spend it on the company site. This currency could also be used on other online sites. Stores that participated in this received bonuses, so it encouraged more stores to be part of their campaign.

It cost $1 million to market, which included Whoopi Goldberg as their spokesperson. The premise was good and popular enough, so much so that it raised venture capital to the tune of $35 million (Rossen, 2017).

Unfortunately, it was not sustainable and cost the company heavily. Not all the stores participated, which led to the company making a deal with the vendors guaranteeing its transactions, regardless of whether they were fraudulent or not. This led to Russian and Philippine hackers using stolen credit cards on the Flooze.com platform to make purchases, which caught the eye of the FBI. It was not safe and secure, which made it open to scammers that crippled it enough that it closed down.

A lot of the ideas that are used in cryptocurrency today are taken from that attempt, which had great promise but terrible timing.

Digicash

An American cryptographer named David Chaum came up with the concept of a token that could be safely passed between individuals and replace currency.

It was encrypted using what he called a 'blinding formula' or Blind Signature Technology and he published a scientific paper on it in 1983. That means that the token would have a signature of authenticity and could be modified without being traced, even for banks or governments.

Chaum created Digicash in 1989 so that he could use this formula, but unfortunately it didn't stick and so the company went bankrupt in 1998. It seemed too complicated and investors weren't ready to support something so risky in their eyes, especially as e-commerce was too alien to them at the time.

That doesn't mean it was all in vain, as many of the Digicash concepts and formulas and encryption tools played a role in the current digital currency development.

B-Money

Also in 1998, an anonymous, distributed electronic cash system called B-money was proposed by developer Wei Dai.

Dai suggested that two different protocols be used, making B-money very different from Bitcoin in structure. B-money was similar to Bitcoin in what it stood for: to have a secure, private system to transfer money through a decentralized network without the use of a third party.

B-money didn't take off, despite the whitepaper written on it, because investors were not ready to take a chance on such a thing and it wasn't exciting enough for people to pay attention to at the time. To his credit though, Wei Dan's B-money was referenced in the Bitcoin whitepaper because of the impact it had on Bitcoin's creation.

PayPal

The 1990s saw the rise of many startups and a large chunk of those were formed on a similar premise to that of Digicash. The most popular was PayPal, which is still being used today. It was one of the first to allow for online payments, doing so by allowing individuals to transfer money via web browsers quickly and securely.

PayPal then connected with eBay, which was a great move as it didn't just grow its user base but the company itself. That is why it is still popular. PayPal is backed by countries around the world and is a popular platform for freelancers to receive payment for work done.

PayPal is so established these days as something most of us use that it is odd to think that a few decades ago, it was revolutionary!

E-Gold

Inspired by PayPal's web base technique, E-gold dealt with the trading of gold online and then included junk silver and other precious metals. In exchange for these items, users of the platform were offered online credit. It was quite popular, especially because onshore approval in the United States was not needed.

Launched in 1996, E-gold was also not secure enough and its popularity attracted organized crime syndicates that used malware and phishing scams to attack the company.

Things got so bad that the United States federal government had to shut it down in 2005.

BitGold

Although it has a similar name to gold, BitGold didn't deal with gold exchange. Its name comes from the need for the currency to reflect real gold. It was a move to decentralize currency. The concept was proposed around the same time as B-money, 1998, by Nick Szabo.

This computer scientist, legal scholar, and cryptographer designed BitGold so that computers would be involved in solving cryptographic puzzles: in other words, very complicated puzzles that are impossible for a human to solve. The puzzles solved would go to a secure encrypted registry and the solver would get a public key. And then a new puzzle would start based on the prior solve, thus creating a chain. This practice is the basis for crypto-mining today.

Despite it just being a concept, BitGold has been the base of a lot of digital currencies that are available today. Many have ironed out the bugs and structured their currencies around BitGold.

Hash Cash

Adam Black, a British cryptographer and cypherpunk (someone who advocates for privacy and cryptography for political change) created this piece of software in 1997.

The purpose of Hash Cash was to stop spam emails and denial of service attacks via a proof-of-work system. What this means is that one party needs to prove that the work done by the computer is correct, and this is done with a lot of backend programming involving cryptography. So, once again, difficult puzzles are solved by computers: a pattern emerges.

This software is still around. In fact, it is used in cryptocurrency and especially Bitcoin as part of their mining structure. You will read about mining later in this chapter.

What Is Blockchain?

Blockchain is a type of database. That means it is an organized collection of information, that can be accessed via a computer system, and is very specific in the way it stores its information. Think of a storage warehouse for information that is organized well and has a different layout from other storage warehouses.

Blockchains are known for being secure databases because data can't be altered, deleted, or replaced.

New data is stored in a new block, which is chained onto the next block in chronological order: hence, the name *blockchain*. Each block has a timestamp so that it can follow chronological order.

The most common type of information stored are ledgers for transactions. Think of virtual ledgers or books containing transactions in them. Other types of information can be stored on the blockchain as well, it just depends on how the software is being used.

With Bitcoin, it is decentralized, meaning that all users have control, not just a single user or group. This makes the data irreversible so that transactions are permanently recorded and anyone who is a user can view them securely without anything being changed fraudulently.

All businesses rely on information; this information is the data that needs to be stored in a database. But not just stored: it needs to be done fast and as accurately as possible without anything being changed in the process. Blockchain allows businesses to do various activities, like track orders, production lines, or even check for proof of identity fast and efficiently.

It is difficult for scammers to cheat the system because it's so secure that ownership can't be changed, only tracked. And there are no third parties involved who could change data on the route from one user to the next.

Companies That Currently Use Blockchain Technology

Blockchain technology is used by various companies, not just cryptocurrencies like Bitcoin. Since it is a secure database, it has other uses that companies around the world are taking an interest in. The technology is no longer experimental and full of risk, and as it evolves, so does technology as a whole.

Big companies don't want to be left behind and have whole departments dedicated just to blockchain technology.

IBM

IBM uses blockchain to trace how food products get to its locations with IBM Food Trust. This application was created because of the large number of diseases and hazardous material being introduced to foods after leaving the warehouse.

Having to discard contaminated food was costing companies a lot of money, as well as the trust of consumers who were affected. Now, instead of taking weeks to investigate what went wrong, IBM can track food distribution in real-time. The blockchain technology has helped with food safety and the safety of consumers.

Blockchain technology was used to track data from IoT devices across the journey the food was taking to determine where things were going wrong. IoT refers to the 'internet of things' and just means the devices have technology that can communicate data like security systems or sensors. The application is so popular that companies with thousands of trucks and deliveries scheduled have started using it.

Shell

Blockchain is being used as a platform for the trade and settlement of crude oil.

Shell is moving away from traditional paper contracts and is using the VAKT blockchain platform to create a smart system that is digital and secure. It is also using Komgo SA so that trade agreements can be done together.

Shell has created a team called Shell's Blockchain Centre of Intelligence, whose purpose—besides the ones mentioned above—is to partner with other Shell businesses to incorporate blockchain technology and build on the tools and skills they have.

Amazon Web Services

Blockchain tools are offered as software packages for companies that don't want to or can't build their own. There are several software blockchain packages to suit specific company needs and can be purchased as part of a subscription, with technical customer support also offered.

This is being done via Amazon's AWS (Amazon Web Services) Marketplace so companies have a variety of options to choose from or can contact the company for help in navigating these.

For example, Nestle had used one such software package when launching a new coffee brand. It allows customers to scan a QR code to see which farm their beans were planted in and where they were then roasted. This way, consumers can track the coffee beans' journey and thus make sustainable decisions when buying coffee.

Anthem

This health insurance company has been using blockchain since 2019. They use it to allow patients to securely access and share their medical data online. Users can use the app on their smartphones, scan the QR code, and have the ability to grant access to their health records to a range of different healthcare providers.

It is still new so that only a few members are using it, but the company is confident that in 3 years all of its 40 million members will have access to this feature.

Once it is fully launched and in use, Anthem plans on using the technology for more than a dozen new projects.

BMW

The luxury car-maker BMW is a member, along with Honda and Ford, of the Mobile Open Blockchain Initiative (MOBI). This means that the auto industry was able to start giving new cars a digital identity in July 2019 via its blockchain vehicle identity standard. It's predicted that, in the future, the technology will be able to track the car's life and share information. This information could be used to make cars better.

MOBI is focused on using blockchain technology to make mobility services greener. more affordable, less congested, and safer by working with not just car manufacturers, but companies and governments as well.

On its own, BMW runs a pilot program with suppliers in Europe and the United States to track materials, components, and parts across the supply chain. It's called PartChain and is being rolled out to more suppliers.

General Electric

Via its Aviation subsidiary, General Electric has built a 'back-to-birth' record of an airplane engine. This record holds details from the manufacturing process as well as the maintenance that was performed. It prevents engines from not being used if there is incomplete paperwork, which is a huge issue in the industry. Now there is a digital paper trail for these parts that allow for trade to continue.

Since starting this, the company has been investing heavily in blockchain technologies to push its business into the future.

JP Morgan

Even one of America's biggest banks uses blockchain. Via its Interbank Information Network, cross-border payments that normally take up to 2 weeks are now done in minutes.

It is called Confirm and is expected to reduce rejected or returned transactions caused by payment details, which in turn lowers the costs from both the sending and receiving banks. The information is checked before anything gets processed, limiting errors and allowing payments to get processed faster.

JP Morgan has stated that 100 institutions use this blockchain via a shared ledger, which is why delays are resolved so quickly.

NASDAQ

NASDAQ was an early adopter of blockchain, having used it since 2015 with plenty of products released and counting. A big product was an electronic voting tool for South Africa's central securities depository in 2017. This meant that voters could vote remotely using an app, with ease and safety.

It is also branching out into other fields and is quite ahead of the market with its blockchain solutions.

Samsung

Nexledger Universal was created so that individuals who wanted to execute agreements can prove their identity with ease and without delay.

It's currently being used by 18 Korean banks via an application called BankSign. People use this app to let banks identify them, even when it isn't their own bank that they are visiting. It is so popular that 235,000 people have signed up for it to date (del Castillo, 2021).

The Samsung Group is also using Nexledger Universal to prove patient identities to speed up health insurance claims, among other things.

United Nations

This is proof that any organization can benefit from using blockchain technology. The United Nations has over 193 members and to manage them, it utilizes various blockchain applications.

One is used to provide funds to individuals displaced by war. They did so using blockchain-verified iris scans rather than ID cards to prevent warlords from stealing these funds.

Currently, the United Nations has five blockchain projects in the works via their United Nations Innovation Network.

Disadvantages of Blockchain

The advantages to blockchain usage are numerous and encouraging based on how rapidly the technology has grown and still is growing. But it is important to also know what some of the disadvantages and concerns are to keep an open mind.

It will take some time to iron everything out, but even so, with so many companies creating their own platforms, some of these problems shouldn't be a deterrent.

Cost

The technology cost is huge, not to mention implementation, so it isn't viable for smaller businesses to start using blockchain just yet. However, with so many big businesses creating departments and teams just for blockchain technology, it should help offset a lot of the costs in the future.

Illicit Activities

There is a history of illicit activities being done, but only at 2.1% in 2019, which dropped to 0.34% in 2020 (Lennon, 2021). It is far-fetched to assume that criminals wouldn't take advantage of any opportunity for their business ventures, but that doesn't mean the blockchain is entirely their domain.

Global Regulation

There is little regulation of blockchain and its decentralized purpose has made many countries concerned about stability. China, Russia, and Columbia have banned Bitcoin and the other thousands of cryptocurrencies available today.

However, the United States hasn't issued a ban and the federal government has left it up to the various states to apply their own rules and regulations. New York was the first state to start regulation of cryptocurrencies in 2015, with 32 states following suit with a few laws already passed.

Europe only started regulation in 2020 and mostly follows the United States stance of 'to each to their own.'

This has created a lot of gray areas when it comes to global regulation, which is concerning but not enough to stop the technology from being incorporated worldwide.

Self-Maintenance

Users are in charge of their own wallets on the blockchain, which could mean data is lost if you're not careful. If you lose your password and can't recover it, then your data is lost.

It's the same with your crypto wallet: if you lose your key or log-in information, you lose everything, which could be thousands of dollars depending on how far you have gotten with usage.

The same rules apply for internet safety, which is to keep this information safe and offline. And most important of all, practice using two-factor authentication: an electronic method for accessing a website only after two methods are presented and entered. There are various apps to choose from and they are easy to use.

Why Do We Use Cryptocurrencies Today?

Cryptocurrency is used to purchase and sell items like any other currency, and with its growing popularity, more companies are opting in, and for good reason. Here are a few places crypto is being used at the time of writing.

Low-Cost Money Transfers

This just means that for purchasing and selling via transactions, you get what you want in a shorter time. It is also much cheaper because there are no third parties involved, like banks, when it comes to international money transfers. So if you want to buy a couch from a furniture store, you pay for that couch at the price advertised. There are no bank fees or transaction charges involved.

Travel

Certain travel agencies now allow you to use cryptocurrency to book flights, car rentals, and hotel accommodation. You can also convert cryptocurrency when traveling so that you have the local currency on hand.

With there being over 2,500 cryptocurrencies available today that are used worldwide, the travel industry couldn't just pass up this valuable opportunity. As travelers evolve, so too does the industry to keep up.

You can also use Bitcoin to pay for your space travel with Virgin Galactic.

Startup Investments

In the past, only the wealthy and big businesses could invest in startups, but the world has changed drastically. Now, as long as you have enough in your cryptocurrency wallet, you can invest in the startups that you want to see succeed.

Most startups are thrilled with this because it ensures that they can get enough funding without needing the backing of big investors. This has enabled the creation of several companies backed by their supporters and changed how people invest in businesses.

The biggest difference is that the companies are not guaranteed to succeed and these new investors know that. They do it because it is part of investing and growing the industry and quite revolutionary.

Crypto Mining

This started with Bitcoin mining whereby anyone could mine for Bitcoin using the computers they had at home. These computers solved complicated mathematical equations and you were rewarded with a percentage of Bitcoin.

Nowadays there are complicated setups for Bitcoin mining and so it isn't bringing in as much of a passive income as it was 10 years ago. Luckily, more cryptocurrencies allow for passive income earning via mining. Ethereum and NiceHash are the most popular.

Ethereum

To mine Ethereum, you just need a graphics card with more than 4 gigabytes of video memory that you can purchase at any computer shop, an Ethereum wallet by joining up, and your computer of course.

Then, join a mining pool like Ethermine, because you earn as transactions are solved and you can't do that on your own. Next, install the software and start mining.

NiceHash

This is an easy mining platform for those starting out, which is why it's so popular. NiceHash is an app that helps you find mining software and a pool to join. It also pays in Bitcoin, even though you're mining for Ethereum, and has slightly higher fees to use.

Content Payment

There are a couple of companies that will pay for content using cryptocurrency. It all started with a SteemIt, which allows you to earn in two ways: creating original content or interacting with posts via comment or upvoting.

Since its creation in 2017, many other companies have followed suit, like Read.cash, PublishOx, and Honest. DLive does something different because its content isn't about writing but video streaming. The best way to describe it is Youtube with more perks and the pay is cryptocurrency.

There is also blogging, editing, and translation content work that is available on various sites across various cryptocurrencies. It is a wonderfully creative way to reward content writers in the industry.

Why You Should Be Using Cryptocurrency

Why should you use cryptocurrency? It's not as volatile as people think and is a very viable way of trading online.

Coinbase was the first crypto exchange to go public on the NASDAQ and plenty of companies, like Fidelity, are adding cryptocurrencies to their investment offerings. There are several others that you will come across in the next chapter.

Companies are not afraid to expand their portfolios and get with the times because it isn't a bubble; it is here to stay and changing the online world for the better. Online pay systems have been around for years, but with cryptocurrency, it is safer and traceable. And of course, there is also the financial guarantee in NFT trading that will bring you a sizable passive income.

So, it is secure because all transactions are on the ledger and traceable. Being decentralized, it isn't controlled by any government or bank, which means it lowers the risk of identity theft unless you lose your passwords. With so many companies jumping on board, it is easily accessible and you are the owner because there isn't a cash system that your cryptocurrency has to pass through.

Chapter 2:

Fractional Ownership

The concept of fractional ownership is very important to get your head wrapped around before diving into NFT investments. It will give you a better understanding of who owns what when you start trading.

Fractional ownership may sound like a complicated new-fangled concept, but it has been around for a while. How it works is that a high-value item or asset that can be used as a holiday home can be bought by more than one person and the usage is shared.

Using the example of the holiday home, let's say there are four owners. They would equally share the time spent in the holiday home and split the costs for maintenance and upkeep. Rental money would also be split between the owners.

This allows you to own something of high value without breaking the bank, especially as you won't be using it all the time. It is suitable in places that have laws in place that offer benefits for ownership.

History

The concept of fractional ownership started in Europe in the late 1970s under the name 'co-ownership.' It was used in southern France, Spain, Portugal, and the Canary Islands, hence the alternative names of 'co-propriete,' 'co-propiedad,' or 'pro-indiviso."

The usage plans were complex and inflexible, so they didn't last. But in the 1990s it made a comeback and appeared in the United States. More people wanted second homes in areas known to have the best skiing. Since these areas were not affordable to one individual and reservation technology had improved dramatically since the 1970s, many people jumped on the concept. It became so popular that assets started including items like jet aircraft, luxury yachts, classic and supercars, artwork, and more.

The industry exploded over the years and expanded across the world, especially in Southeast Asia (Bali and Thailand). Things only slowed down in 2008 due to the global financial crisis, and have continued to slow. But the industry hasn't stopped, despite the decline in growth. It is predicted to pick up as the global real estate market takes a turn for the better.

Property

Fractional ownership sounds very much like the concept of time-sharing but it isn't, even though the two are often confused. Because of this confusion, rebranding had to take place in the fractional ownership industry to help it stand out. It is different because the owners own a portion of the real estate, not just a time period that they can use it.

A property management company normally oversees the upkeep and maintenance of the property while the owners just pay the bills. So it is part ownership of something with several individuals, not the renting out of the use of that something.

Other Areas of Use

Fractional ownership has been mostly used for real estate, but over the years, the concept has expanded to other items.

Aircraft

Individuals or companies can purchase a share of an aircraft from as little as one-sixteenth up to half. It all depends on how often the owner wants to be able to use the plane and how much they can pay for that usage. They also need to cover a percentage of the aircraft's purchase price while the contract is valid. This type of purchase is different from real estate in that contracts run for 5 years at the most.

All other administrative fees also need to be paid and split between the owners, with each owner being guaranteed a certain number of hours at short notice. This is possible because fractional aircraft owners are not assigned a dedicated aircraft but are given access to a pool of similar makes and models. So, in fact, you own a share of the aircraft company and are entitled to usage of any aircraft in the fleet as per the title or deed from the purchase.

Business Aviation: Jet Aircraft

This was only introduced in 1986 by Richard Santulli, an American Businessman, mathematician, and millionaire. It was done via his company NetJets, to cut down costs after he had a look at the logbooks of pilots over the years. It was very successful and the company expanded into Europe in the 1990s and Russia, becoming the largest business jets operator in Europe by 2006.

In the later years, the company wasn't seeing as much demand but stayed strong in the industry, with an upsurge during the start of the COVID-19 pandemic.

Yacht/Boat Ownership

These include small yachts, cabin cruisers, sportfishing yachts, as well as megayachts. Smaller boats don't cost as much these days, but leave you with limited choice in terms of usage. Bigger, fancier boats are not affordable for one individual.

That's where fractional boat ownership comes in and there are several companies that you can contact to help you find exactly what you want and at what percentage you can afford. These companies are handy in that you are given the monthly budget, including the yearly increased costs, so that you are well aware of all costs involved.

You are also offered benefits, like trading your time for a different boat and place which, depending on the package taken, could be a tropical island in another country!

The contracts are also easy to get out of, as some companies offer exit points if you have been a customer for a certain amount of years. These points can be spent to sell the yacht back to the company instead of looking for a new owner yourself. It's a very cost-effective way of living a luxurious lifestyle on the open sea.

Recreational Vehicles

Recreation vehicles (RVs) or motor homes are very popular in the United States but depreciate by as much as 30% the moment the vehicle is driven off the lot. It is an industry that has needed to be part of the bigger fractional ownership industry.

Today, several companies deal with fractional ownership by state. They will even find people to rent the vehicle out for you so that you make a profit on your investment during your contract. I say 'contract' because, usually, the agreement is about 5 years; then the vehicle is sold and the money is split among the owners. This is normally when you can reinvest in a better model should you wish to do so.

Sports Cars

It was only a matter of time before owning a part of a luxury car was possible. Porsche experimented with this concept in 2018 in Atlanta by offering daily and weekly rentals to see if anyone was keen. It helped increase sales dramatically and many other car companies have now done the same for their brands and for specific models.

Companies have also sprung up that deal purely with fractional luxury car ownership so you have more than just a Porsche to choose from and can have a tailor-made plan to suit your pocketbook.

Artwork

It has become quite evident that for more people to appreciate art, it needs to be more available to collect. And given the high price to own a piece of art, it's no wonder that most people can't afford to do so. Now, more art lovers can own a beautiful piece and start learning about the art collection industry without breaking the bank by owning a share of a piece of art.

This has also enabled established collectors to expand their portfolio and galleries to save on exhibition costs by selling a percentage of high-end pieces.

Chapter 3:

What Are NFTs?

NFTs, also known as *Nyfties* are digital assets on a blockchain. They have unique qualities that stop them from being interchangeable. That means that they are difficult to forge, so it guarantees the authenticity of the item being purchased.

As technology grew, so did the ease of making forgeries, duplicating work, and so forth that have been costing artists their well-earned pay for decades. NFTs have helped to solve the problem artists around the world have been having when it came to getting their well-earned royalties. NFT ownership is recorded on the blockchain, thus preventing illegal copies from being made. This ensures that artists get paid for their work.

Hence, the different types of NFTs springing up, which include music, artwork, event tickets, domain names, physical asset ownership, and collectibles. At the moment these are sold at auctions in a similar style to how artwork is sold at a live auction. The only difference is that it is all done online.

How Does It Work?

NFTs are mostly found on the Ethereum blockchain and Ethereum-based tokens are used to authenticate ownership of the NFT. That's because the item or asset is attached to the token, so you can copy the file from someone else's NFT but it won't be the original and that can be traced. Whoever owns the token owns the NFT. As such, each copy or reproduction is verified as not being the original. The token contains the ownership information, a certificate of authenticity, and copyright information.

The blockchain is the public register for ownership of a digital item that is secure because it can't be hacked or overwritten. A ledger entry is created the same way as with any blockchain cryptocurrency. This entry contains the address to the file, which establishes ownership of the NFT. When the NFT is sold, then that token code is also transferred and noted as a ledger entry. This is how ownership is tracked on the blockchain.

The NFT owner can add metadata to the character of their new NFT. This additional information would describe whether it is art, music, and so forth, as well as what format it is in: for example, jpeg. video, and so on.

Tokens don't have any value on their own; the value is based on the media attached to it. Think of an award-winning piece of art. The artist's talent and reputation give the painting its value and so that is what it gets priced for an auction. Value is based on market demand. It is also based on rarity or scarcity, because the NFT creator can decide if they want to make copies and, if so, how many.

Something very important to bear in mind is that the artist still owns the copyright, which they use to claim their royalties. This is where the previous chapter on fractional ownership comes in handy.

So you own the item but cannot duplicate it. Also, it could be stored on the artist's website, which could be taken down. Therefore, ensure that you know what happens to the asset should these things occur, to protect your purchase.

Why Is It Popular Now?

The amount that several digital items have been sold for has turned heads. And the industry has exploded purely because cryptocurrency is on the rise and the COVID-19 pandemic has pushed a lot of items online. People can't physically watch a concert, so they purchase an exclusive album online and watch it there.

People were also not spending as much money because they were stuck indoors, didn't have to drive to work, and couldn't travel, so they now have the extra cash to spend. Plus, cryptocurrencies have surged in popularity, so one could say that the stars have aligned for NFT trading.

Its popularity has also helped create several companies that facilitate the buying and selling of NFTs, called NFT Marketplaces that we will cover in-depth in Chapter 6.

A lot of investors are paying high rates to promote NFTs based on their belief that they will only increase in profitability.

With all this backing, it's no wonder more people are interested. Add to that the fact that trade is an easy process that doesn't require extra financial backing or extra platforms. For example, if you create a piece of digital art, you just have to sell it on a marketplace. There is no need to market it, spend money on promoting it, or punt potential buyers.

Is It a Crypto Fad?

I have mentioned a few times that NFTs are not new and have been around for at least a decade. An example of this are CryptoKitties, digital kittens that were collectibles, and very popular among those involved in cryptocurrency when they were created in 2017. Despite all the celebrity hype, NFTs aren't a fad based on how high the trading volume is and is still growing.

NFTs have been linked to a technological revolution that taps into us wanting to own rare items of high value without the worry of illegal copies. This is fantastic in an age where everything that is online can and is copied. NFTs bring back value to items with security and traceability.

Even though there were record-making sales in the news, NFT prices have dropped but are staying constant even as the hype dies down, which is making it a much more stable market in which to invest. It's also innovative and new, which can be a push back to many who are presented with something that seems too good to be true.

This is why there are concerns that the NFT market could crash and bring down investors with it. But not everyone is skeptical. NFTs have been likened to the dot-com bubble when people thought the internet was a fad. In reality, it was just overly priced early projects that had caused all the excitement.

At the moment, there is a lot of hype, so prices are high but they will drop and stabilize. This is a good thing because it means that NFT trading is here for the long term.

What Are Speculative Investments?

With any type of investment, you need to do research, so it's important to cover all three types of investments: saving, investing, and speculating.

You will thank me later.

Save

The first way to invest is to *save* by putting money aside. For example, you can put your money into a savings account to save for a specific item. Although you have the value of the item, that can change but not rapidly, and you are saving towards it. The process is slow, with very little growth in terms of interest, but your money is safe because you won't lose any in the process.

This method can be used for short-term usage if you're saving for something specific and don't want to pay a penalty for an early withdrawal from an IRA. But mostly retirement funds for long-term usage are included in these types of investments.

Invest

Investing your money just means that you are taking on a small risk as your money starts growing, based on where it is invested. This is a long-term process with a minimum of 3 years, so that any losses can be offset when the profits increase. Anything shorter and you won't see a good trade-off. That's because your money will rise and fall as markets do but not at a scary rate and by the end, you would have weathered the ups and downs and realized a good profit.

This can be done by owning shares in a business that is successful because you are expecting its success to mean bigger returns for you. Most people will just invest with companies that specialize in this and put the money where they feel it will grow.

Speculate

With speculation you are looking at quick profits over very short periods of time. The risk is significantly higher as you are hoping that you don't lose your money and make a high return. An example of this is day trading.

Speculation has been likened to gambling one's money, but there is an art to speculation and when done right, the rewards are fantastic. The key is to keep an eye on the markets to determine what will bring in the most profit.

This isn't a new concept, as it is used for art, collectibles, stocks, and other tangible items. The only difference now is that the items are digital, not physical, and you can trace its authenticity in a secure environment.

NFTs fall under speculative investment because their value fluctuates, depending on what is popular. It's important to understand this concept well as you begin your journey into NFT trading because the risks are high.

What Are the Most Expensive NFTs to Date?

As the list is continuously changing, I am not going to list the top 10 most expensive NFTs to date, but I will list some of the most *notable* NFTs to date, not just based on their price but also on their rarity and originality.

Beeple With Everydays: The First 5,000 Days

This piece of NFT art was sold at Christie's for $69 million and to date is the largest amount anyone has paid for an NFT, as well as the most expensive work of art by a living artist. It is made up of 500 pieces of art that had been created in May 2007.

The artwork was bought by Vignesh Sundaresan, also known as MetaKovan, who has displayed it in a digital art museum in the Metaverse, which is a virtual space that is shared.

Edward Snowden with Stay Free (Edward Snowden 2021)

This piece of art depicts Edward Snowden's portrait over the court documents showing that the National Security Agency in the United States illegally mass surveyed individuals. This was a piece of charity art that benefited a company called Freedom of the Press Foundation by being sold for over $5.4 million.

Mad Dog Jones With Replicator

This artist is currently the most-expensively selling living Canadian artist because of this piece of art. It is also unique in that new NFTs will come from it every 28 days, each with its own resale value. This is quite a return on investment for the buyer, who could own up to 220 unique NFTs that they can sell. Well worth the cost of $4.1 million if you can get so much more out of it, don't you think?

Kevin McCoy With Quantum

This is an exceptionally unique NFT, as it is the first-ever created as far back as 2014. The artist created the token on Namecoin in May 2014 using technology he created with the coder Anil Dash. They presented this to an audience at the New Museum in New York but their audience laughed.

But as the phrase goes, "Who's laughing now?" I would say $1.4 million is certainly having the two creators laughing all the way to the bank.

Pak With the Switch

This piece of artwork gives the owner the option of changing the artwork to a new unknown image. This is part of the artist's way of representing the way art is evolving digitally. However, once the new owner decides to trigger the switch, then it can't be changed back.

It was sold as part of a collection of seven pieces of digital art at Sotheby's for $17 million, so I can see why the owner would be hesitant to change the piece.

3LAU With Gunky's Uprising

This piece is a combination of animated artwork and a music video created to celebrate the disc jockey (DJ) and electronic musician's third anniversary of his album *Ultraviolet*. For $1.3 million, it's no wonder he has a couple more art pieces for sale.

These feature unreleased music with the option for the buyer to name the songs as well, when purchased.

Don Diablo With Destination Hexagonia

This Dutch DJ, record producer, musician, and songwriter is known for his electronic music created this full-length, 1-hour concert.

Based on a Sci-Fi theme, the owner received a hard drive containing the only copy of the file. This makes it a very rare collectible, and worth the roughly $1.2 million cost.

Don Diablo is now creating NFT comic books.

Larva Labs With CryptoPunks

These NFTs, inspired by the London punk scene, the cyberpunk movement, and several books and movies, were released on the Ethereum blockchain in 2017.

These are limited to 10,000 characters (6,039 males and 3,840 females) and created through computer code so no two characters are duplicated. Some have even rarer traits, which makes them great collectibles. These traits include humans, zombies, apes, and alien CryptoPunks, the latter three being the rarest and most valuable.

This is especially true now, with the boom in NFT sales. A couple of years ago, they could be obtained for free by anyone with an Ethereum wallet. Now they are being purchased for as much as $7.58 million each.

Jack Dorsey With the First-Ever Tweet

Jack Dorsey, the CEO of Twitter, has also jumped on the bandwagon and sold his and Twitter's first-ever tweet for $2.9 million. The tweet was sent on March 6, 2006 and went on sale via the platform Valuables. It was purchased by a Malaysian-based businessman who coveted the purchase and likened it to owning Da Vinci's *Mona Lisa*.

This is exactly how NFTs are perceived: valuable pieces of artwork that are rare.

Sky Mavis With Axie Infinity

This online video game uses Ethereum cryptocurrency that allows players to trade, collect, breed, raise, and battle creatures called 'axies.' All the characters are NFTs and in February 2021, an estate from the game was sold for $1.5 million: virtual estate from a video game.

This made it the largest digital land sale recorded on the blockchain.

Chapter 4:

How NFTs Are Used

NFTs are mainly used to sell exclusive, digital items online, so it is a graphics interchange format (GIF) file or a domain name that you have the token and location for but can't physically touch.

NFTs have the potential to verify physical items for proof of ownership. Items like artwork and property fall into this category.

Real Estate

Since NFTs contain the digital certificate as proof of ownership that can't be forged or lost, it has become quite popular in the world of real estate and is looking to become the industry standard for such transactions.

First, NFTs combine the proof-of-ownership, contractual terms of what can be done to the property, and the basis for buying and selling into one package instead of being split into three, as with a conventional deed.

Second, it removes the need for brokers so properties are more accessible online, not to mention the security and traceability of transactions.

It's not just a concept also, the world's first real estate NFT was successfully sold in 2021. It's an apartment in Kyiv, Ukraine, which made history in 2017 by being the first property to be sold and bought using blockchain technology. The now previous owner decided to sell it as an NFT to showcase the benefits of blockchain technology in the real estate industry.

Three things were included in the NFT: access to the ownership paperwork, a picture of the apartment, and another NFT in the form of digital art by a popular artist. The physical painting of this art was painted on the wall of the apartment and can be seen in the picture of the apartment.

This was an international sale because the property is in the Ukraine but the new owner is based in America. So the property had to be held and recorded in the Ukraine as a United States limited liability company (LLC) first. The NFT contained rights to the LLC, so the new owner had a smooth transfer process.

This sale has now paved the way for future real estate transactions.

Virtual Worlds

There are whole worlds created that you can wander through, create, and purchase items in. It's similar to playing an online video game that is played in real time and you are the main character. They have become popular because physical distance isn't a deterrent for connection and interaction.

In these virtual worlds, trading digital assets has seen a boom and make up 20% of the NFT market to date. Real estate purchases are made regularly in these worlds in the form of NFTs, ranging from $1.5 million to $2.8 million worth of land.

Many of you might be unfamiliar with the concept of 'virtual reality,' let alone virtual worlds, so I will explain this in more detail.

Virtual Reality

The concept of virtual reality was something you would find in science fiction books depicting a world full of robots and flying cars. But these days it is very much part of the world and the technology is improving constantly.

Virtual reality is a simulation, an imitation of an experience that could be from the real world, like climbing a mountain, or completely different, like a sword fight on a ship in the open seas. It's not just used for entertainment but also education, in terms of military or medical training, like flight simulators for pilots, or virtual business meetings that have soared during the Covid-19 pandemic.

We have all attended at least one ZOOM call where someone has a virtual background, like a beach in Bali when you know they live in an apartment in Brooklyn.

The technology now includes augmented reality (interaction with objects from real-world environments) and mixed reality (interaction with real and virtual worlds), referred to as 'extended reality.'

Movies like *Tron*, *Johnny Mnemonic*, and *The Matrix* are great examples of this, if not a little outdated.

Equipment

The first mounted virtual reality system was available in the 1960s, continued into the 1980s with a couple of commercial products, before tapering off. From 2010 onward it has fast-tracked, with the creation of Oculus Rift that took years in the making until its launch in 2016.

The device looks like a thick pair of goggles that go over your eyes and that must be connected to a computer or your cell phone. The user also needs to have on headphones, and you use hand controllers and other accessories to navigate. Think of moving around in a dream but having control over your actions.

Oculus Rift is a line of virtual reality headsets that are now discontinued, to make way for its successors, with the latest model being Oculus Quest 2, in operation since October 13, 2020. This headset allows the user to enter a virtual world: either one that is fantasy-based or based on reality, like mountain-climbing games. It is meant to fully immerse the user so that they think they are in that world, experiencing everything.

There is even Samsung Gear VR, which fits around Samsung smartphones to create a cheaper virtual reality experience. The range is huge and caters to various tastes and budgets, as various companies have started creating their own products.

The Metaverse

The metaverse refers to virtual worlds that are shared. The word itself is used to describe what the internet is setting out to be. It was first used in the book *Snow Crash* by Neal Stephenson in 1992, which depicted a virtual world with which users could interact.

With the popularity of NFTs growing and the creation of so many virtual worlds for people to interact with, the technology is looking to be able to merge these two, so that they are all shared.

The current owner of the most expensive NFT to date, the artwork *Everydays: The First 5,000 Days*, plans on exhibiting this in four virtual worlds so that it can be viewed and enjoyed by people in more than one place.

And within these virtual worlds products of all kinds are being bought and sold. Even companies like Taco Bell are and have been developing products for this market. It's a very different kind of retail.

Decentraland

Decentraland is the most popular virtual world to date. It is community-based and allows its users to own plots of land, artwork, and NFTs in the form of various things, which include collectibles. Users also get to participate in its governance.

It started out in 2016 using a 2D model, but is now one of the largest 3D worlds out there. It has its own cryptocurrency, called 'mana' that, along with the game's assets, is located on Ethereum's blockchain.

Decentraland is different from other online games because the players control the rules of play. When you join, you also join the Decentralized Autonomous Organization (DAO), which allows you to vote on various things to change the structure or policies of the game. There is a marketplace for the selling and buying of NFTs that range from in-game collectibles, from clothes to land. You can display your

NFT art, trade items, and even monetize your land; the options are endless.

As mentioned above regarding the Metaverse, within these virtual worlds products of all kinds are being bought and sold. In Decentraland Adidas put on a fashion show and designs were sold as NFTs in. Now more, fashion houses and sports brands are putting on shows and advertising their virtual designs.

Loans

You can now borrow money using an NFT as collateral. There are a few marketplaces, like Hoard Exchange, that are running beta websites for this function and several financial institutions, like Lamna Financial in South Africa, that have started to offer NFT loans.

The reasoning is based on the surge of cryptocurrency and digital technology so clients are changing how they do things. To keep up, financial institutions don't want to be left behind.

Types of NFTs

There are various types of NFTs, with more being created all the time, because the possibilities are truly endless. Anything you could think of could be an NFT or is already.

Art

Art are the most common forms of NFTs and range from digital designs, videos, GIFs, photographs, memes, social media content, and pixels. We will talk more about this type in later chapters and how you can trade in this type of NFT successfully.

Articles

Several articles from the *New York Times* and *Quartz* have been sold as NFTs. One was from journalist Kevin Roose, who wrote an article about selling the article then auctioned it as an NFT for $560,000.

Although not a news article, it's worth mentioning that the first news organization to sell its artwork was The Associated Press, for $180,000. It was called, *The Associated Press calls the 2020 presidential election on blockchain—A view from Outer Space.*

Quartz's article was the first agency to sell an article, and that went for $1,814.

Music

The band Kings of Leon was the first to release their album as an NFT in March 2021, and generated a cool $2 million for the band. They were not the only ones though; plenty of musicians have been digitizing their work because of this new revenue stream.

Linkin Park's Mike Shinoda, Grimes, DJ Steve Aoki, and many more have since been using various marketplace platforms to get their art to fans and have seen excellent returns.

Trading Cards

These are digital versions of physical collectibles cards, like baseball cards or tabletop gaming cards.

Sports

The first in the sports world to start was the NBA, with NFTs containing highlights of fans' favorite basketball teams. These were packaged like digital trading cards and were a huge hit, and still are with over $390 million made since their October 2020 launch.

Now you can find NFTs in boxing and Formula 1, among other sports that are also taking an interest.

Metaverse/Video Games

We touched on the metaverse and virtual reality worlds, like Decentraland, whereby NFTs are abundant in all forms. The most common, though, are those that make the gaming experience more enjoyable. Things like avatars, which are video game characters created by the user to look like whatever they want, allow the player to change their appearance as much as they want. You can also get skins that change the appearance of the avatar but don't affect the gameplay in any way, like getting a haircut.

Finally, there are collectibles that are often hidden items that give users a bonus of some sort, like a sword or gun. These are not required to complete game stages but do add great bonuses and are worth the find.

Fashion

Following the same premise as avatar clothing, designer fashion houses have started offering digital luxury fashion items. For those that can afford it, it is now possible for your virtual self to own a pair of Gucci sneakers. And it isn't a crazy concept, because high fashion is all about identity and exclusivity. Now it is possible to celebrate that ideal in a virtual world as well.

The world's first virtual mall was created on June 29, 2021, and allows customers to browse virtual stores and make purchases. It is called Metajuka and is expanding as more fashion houses and designers join in the NFT fashion frenzy.

Domain Names

In the past, an organization controlled the buying and selling of domain names, but now all the new owner needs are the private keys in the NFT.

Domain names relating to cryptocurrency are very popular and go for a lot of money, because everyone wants to own one. Of course, NFT domain names are all the rage now because you can't get into the market if you don't have the right name. The most expensive domain name was "win.crypto," which was sold for $100,000 by Unstoppable Domain.

The technology here is also growing because domain names can link crypto wallets, thus making it easier to send and receive cryptocurrency.

Film

The digital posters from *Deadpool 2* were sold in March 2021, as well as the Oscar-nominated *Claude Lanzmann: Spectres of the Shoah*. The latter was the first motion picture, documentary, and Oscar-nominated film to be turned into an NFT and auctioned.

But that isn't all from the film industry. Anthony Hopkins' new movie *Zero Contact* will premier as an NFT on the Vuele platform, which will be the first time that this is done. This is indeed something to look forward to, as there will be more than one copy but each will be unique in terms of the extras and at different prices. The director, Rick Dugdal, has stated that this means the movie is being released as a 'limited edition.'

Memes

If you haven't come across memes, they are ideas, behaviors, or styles in the form of humorous images that are passed on via social media. Several popular memes have been minted as NFTs and sold, like *Doge* (an image of a Shiba Inu dog), *Nyan Cat*, and *Disaster Girl*, for as much as $4 million each.

The reason for this is quite simple: wealthy collectors want to collect early internet history but not just how it looked when it went viral, but how it originated and from the source. That's why the famous meme of the gorilla Harambe was tracked down and the photographer, Jeff McCurry, is about to make history by selling the original photograph as an NFT.

Pornography

Popular porn stars have also started to convert their work into NFTs as part of creating unique content for their customers. Other NFT marketplaces haven't been very supportive of this and the industry as a whole, but these NFTs do exist. As a result, marketplaces for this type of NFT have been springing up and holding their own auctions, thus creating a new niche in the adult industry.

Academia

Research funding isn't always easy to come by so Yale's Department of Statistics and Data Science (S&DS) has come up with a solution: auditioning its first NFT. It was created to honor *Anscombe's Quartet*, Francis Anscombe's classic research piece. published in 1973. He was the founding chair at the Yale Department of Statistics. It's most commonly used to teach researchers about why graphing data before analyzing is important.

It's not the only bit of academia being minted as an NFT. The patent disclosures for CRISPR-Cas9 gene editing and cancer immunotherapy have been minted as NFTs by the University of California Berkeley and sold for $55,000 on June 8, 2021.

This is paving the way for more research papers to bring in needed funding.

Social Tokens

These are tokens issued by individuals and communities and based on a brand, community, or influencer. Some have used it for their time, such as an hour's worth of consulting. Others have used it to reward follower engagement.

It is a way for celebrities and influencers to monetize their time with their fans or followers and is a very lucrative way to earn money by popularity.

Chapter 5:

How Are NFTs Created?

Many NFTs are created on the Ethereum blockchain, using its ETH currency to pay for its use. But that doesn't mean these have to keep moving around to get sold. The NFT is held in a virtual wallet that goes with the person to different platforms, allowing them access to this wallet. An application like MetaMask is needed so that each platform can access this wallet for any buying and selling to take place smoothly.

Various marketplaces allow you to create NFTs without paying any fees, like OpenSea and Mintbase. Each of these has its own set of step-by-step instructions on how to use the site.

Most marketplace platforms charge you a fee, called 'gas fees' for the cost of creation or minting of the NFT. These charges change frequently and can be pricey. But once these fees are paid and the NFT is uploaded to a site, then it has been created and is ready to be sold.

History and Key Concepts

Most books and articles talk about the popularization of NFTs and their beginnings, starting with CryptoKitties. I did the same a few chapters ago. But the concept was conceived much earlier so now I am going to take you on that journey. Let's dive into the history of NFTs and the key concepts that make these NFTs what they are today.

Bitcoin Colored Coins

Bitcoin colored coins were used in 2012 to trade meme artwork. They were also known as 'satoshis,' the smallest unit of Bitcoin and equivalent to one-hundredth of a Bitcoin. They were also named after Bitcoin's creator, Satoshi Nakamoto.

These colored coins were only used in very small circles and, hence, were relatively unheard of. They didn't last long because they could only represent a value if everyone agreed on that value. This caused major transaction issues when an agreement couldn't be reached.

Quantum

In Chapter 3 I mentioned a piece of artwork called *Quantum* that was sold for a hefty price. Well, that piece of artwork is based on what is considered to be the first NFT.

Kevin McCoy and Anil Dash created a platform for digital art to exist. They did this in 2014 and presented their idea, but it didn't take. It's for this reason that they never patented their blockchain idea and why they don't own the technology today.

They are not forgotten though, and Anil Dash is still around in cryptocurrency and startup circles. He doesn't want to sell the original presentation video as an NFT just yet. But Kevin McCoy was quite prepared to sell *Quantum*, which is acknowledged for what it is and how it helped with the technology and ultimate NFT creation.

CounterParty

CounterParty is a financial platform that was peer-to-peer and built on the blockchain in 2014. It dealt with memes and card games trading. The company was created because the creators believed in blockchain technology but didn't fathom how big a part it would play.

When memes started being sold, starting with Pepe Frog between 2015 and 2016, CounterParty saw a rise in users. This spurred rare images of this meme becoming the thing to collect, and people were quite prepared to spend a lot of money to own a rare Pepe Frog. It was this popularity that convinced the creators of Force of Will to collaborate on the platform in 2016.

Force of Will was a popular trading card game at the time and they needed a place to sell their cards. This brought in another surge of sales, ultimately showcasing the value of being able to buy and sell such collections online and with ease.

Ethereum

Ethereum was created in 2017 as not just a cryptocurrency but much more. The company made its own headlines based on what it was able to do, but things truly started taking off with the release of CryptoKitties. This was an NFT game on the Ethereum platform that allowed its users to breed rare digital cats using blockchain technology.

The popularity of the game was the catalyst for NFTs to start taking center stage. It was so popular that it brought with it a lot of media attention, and in a sense started getting more people interested in online collecting.

This gave rise to CryptoPunks and now the list is endless as to what you can buy and sell on various marketplace platforms, depending on what you want to collect.

Carbon Emission Issue

I can't talk about how NFTs are created without touching on the carbon emission issue. It would be irresponsible of me to not talk about it because you will come across it when you start trading in NFTs or even in any discussion concerning cryptocurrency.

NFTs require a lot of computing power because they are created using blockchain transactions that follow the proof-of-work protocol. This simply means that one party proves to the other that a certain amount of work was done. It is proven by solving a mathematical problem or transaction. It sounds complex and it is. However, all of this solving is done with computers that run these equations in the background, with the help of specific software. By solving these equations the people running these computers or miners get rewarded in cryptocurrency, so that is the incentive to have a lot of computers running all the time.

The transactions are solved at a rapid pace, which has given rise to server farms created just for this purpose around the world. Electricity generation at server farms is mostly powered by fossil fuels because they are mostly located in countries with cheap electricity costs. This in turn creates a huge carbon footprint, which is causing a lot of NFT usage pushback. It's the main reason that many people are hesitant to create and sell NFTs despite their popularity.

Ethereum mining is said to consume as much electricity as the country of Ireland and a study done in 2018 found that cryptocurrency mining consumes more energy than extracting gold or copper (de la Garza, 2021).

Even with these studies, it is difficult to calculate exactly what the carbon footprint of an NFT is because there are so many factors to consider. Blockchain miners, who are the ones running these computers, are located all over the world, so it is difficult to pinpoint just how much energy is being used at any given time. So calculating the carbon footprint for each NFT is impossible to determine at the moment. That doesn't mean that there is no impact or that it is not a cause for concern.

It is quite a big talking point, especially with regards to climate change. The consensus is that the power being used needs to be green. Cryptocurrency companies are in agreement, and most are doing a lot to make changes. There are even marketplace platforms that are green and market themselves this way.

A few solutions are also being investigated by companies like the Ethereum platform to change the way the currency is mined and for its carbon footprint to be decreased drastically.

Green Concepts

All mining could be done using renewable resources, but there are various reasons as to why it's not. The biggest reason is that there are a lot of countries that use fossil fuels and the electricity put out is very cheap. That's why a lot of server farms are based in those countries: that, and the incentive to mine is a huge reward. It would be difficult to shut these mining operations down and force them to use solar or wind power because of the infrastructure costs to build these renewable energy options.

So newer blockchain technologies have started implementing alternative validation protocols, like proof-of-stake, which uses a lot less energy per transaction. Ethereum is looking to replace mining with staking, which is much less energy-intensive. As much as 99.98% of energy will be saved once it gets this concept to be used for all its transactions (Ethereum, n.d.)

Luckily, this isn't just a future concept because the technology is being built and used in other platforms at a smaller scale. It just needs to be able to sustain the bigger transactions and work in the backend.

Proof-of-Stake

I explained how the proof-of-work protocol works and how cryptocurrency companies are looking to replace this high-energy concept with proof-of-stake. But what is proof-of-stake?

Transactions still need to be validated for new blocks to be created; that doesn't change. But the validation of these transactions doesn't need vast mining capacity because the energy consumption is low. The hardware required to do these transactions are also low; thus, the low-energy consumption and validators receive transaction fees, not block rewards, so the rewards are different, scalable, and don't promote large server farm mining.

How it works is that validators need to stake a certain amount of cryptocurrency to become a validator. For Ethereum, that amount is 32 ETH and then random validators are chosen to either create a new block or to check and confirm other blocks.

There are penalties too. These penalties encourage good validator behavior and do not reward high computation power. Validators lose a portion of their stake if they fail to do the work or do it badly.

A huge security plus of using this type of validation is that the blockchain is not susceptible to a 51% attack. This can only happen if a miner or mining pool controls 51% of the network's transaction-solving power and then starts creating fraudulent blocks that benefit itself and invalidating those that don't. With proof-of-stake, no one, not even a hacker, would be able to own 51% of the cryptocurrency network and even if they do, there wouldn't be any point in attacking since that would attack their share as well.

Off-Chain Transactions

Off-chain transactions refer to transactions that take place outside of the blockchain. They can work by swapping private keys to an existing wallet or using a third party. This is what PayPal does to honor its transactions.

Off-chain transactions can be done immediately, with no transaction fees and better security. But at some point, these do need to be added to the blockchain to be recorded on the ledger. So there is a cost, but it's not huge.

The biggest tradeoff for this at the moment is that it sacrifices trustworthiness, transparency, and decentralization, everything for which the blockchain and cryptocurrency were created.

Chapter 6:

Creating NFTs

Now that you know how it all started and how it works, you can start creating your own NFTs. I will first take you through the steps needed to get started as a digital artist. Selling this piece of artwork will be covered later in this chapter.

How to Become a Crypto Artist

Just because you didn't start out as a digital artist doesn't mean it's impossible. It can be harder when you are not well known, but I have some hints and tips that might help with that as well.

Not a Digital Artist

If you are a physical artwork artist, then you need to learn the tools and get the software before you can even think of creating NFTs. There is a range to choose from, depending on what devices you will be using and whether you want to eventually print the artwork as well.

Some people have taken their physical art and run it through software to add animations before turning these into NFTs, so that is also an option available to you if you don't want to take the time to learn about tools and creating a digital portfolio from scratch.

Turning Physical Art Into NFTs

You can also skip all of that, because it is possible to sell your physical art as an NFT.

You do need to identify if the physical copy is the unique asset, the digital one, or both. Both can be sold as unique products, but how you list them is very important. The reason for this is that NFTs are unique pieces, and that is why they are sold for a lot of money. It's the rarity value that they bring that makes them collectible.

So one option is to destroy the physical artwork after digitizing it, which is a common practice and creates more value to the NFT. You could also just declare the original as a tool that was part of the creation process and not for sale. There are a lot of options, it just depends on what you want to do.

The equipment needed is a digital SLR camera because this will give you the highest quality, so investing in this piece of equipment is vital. You could also hire a photographer instead of buying your own equipment. Make sure there is a lot of natural light or good lighting.

You could also scan your art using specific software and a specialized scanner to digitize that scan. This is only possible if your artwork is small enough to be scanned and must be scanned at a high dot-per-inch setting.

Already a Digital Artist

These steps are for someone who knows how to use digital artwork tools already and just needs to transition them into NFTs.

If you are already a digital artist then you should already have an artist name or brand. This is important when creating NFTs in a later step. If not, now is a good time to come up with something catchy as a name or brand, but that you doubt will change in the future. You really don't want to use your own name; stick to a pseudonym that you like and would be happy to have for years to come.

The next step is deciding on what you want to create. You should have an idea based on work you've already created, regardless of not having sold anything commercially. A great way to figure this out is to organize your physical artwork and categorize it in terms of genre, style, message, whatever suits you really. Then, either choose your best piece or create a new piece based on your strong points.

Once you have chosen your piece, then decide on the format, as in GIFs, videos, motion graphics, and so forth. Basically, will it just be a piece of digital art or will it be animated or in motion?

Now you can start creating your masterpiece, then uploading it to a marketplace. I will take you through these steps later in the chapter. After you have created your NFT on a marketplace platform of your choice, then there are two very important steps you need to take as an artist starting out: joining a community and promoting your art.

Joining a Community

This is very important for new artists because you will gain valuable knowledge on things like new technologies, market developments, and any trends that might be helpful to how you want your art to evolve.

Join places like Crypto Arts, Arts Rights, and Art Concierge because they support new artists. You are going to need this support to get your art out there and bring in the sales.

Promoting Your Digital Art

Besides getting community assistance, use your social media accounts and friends and family to get the word out. You won't start off making millions, but the point is to create a fanbase and then you will see how well your art will start selling.

Success Stories

A lot of artists from all ages and countries have found this to be quite a profitable venture after years of struggle. Their stories are quite inspiring and each is unique.

Blacksneakers

Jazmine Boykins, a student at North Carolina A&T State University used to post her artwork online for free. The only money that came in was from selling swag at her university. Now her artwork sells for thousands of dollars as NFTs and she has made $60,000 in 6 months.

Her online handle is Blacksneakers and the revenue has given her the confidence to keep going.

Andrew Benson

Based in Los Angeles, Andrew Benson kept his day job because, even though his work made it to museums and he worked with musicians, he wasn't earning enough for him to quit his day job at a software company.

When the pandemic hit, Benson's plans to exhibit fell through, making him doubt that this was all worth it. In January 2021 his friend, who works at Foundation, asked him to submit a piece. It was sold within 10 days for $1, 250. That inspired Benson to submit 10 more pieces that have all sold along the same price range. It would appear his future is looking brighter.

Trevor Jones

This artist from Canada struggled for years and became an artist quite late in his life. Even so, Trevor Jones kept trying to break into the art world, and only in his 40s was he able to start doing artwork based on technology. This was part of finding his niche, and find it he did.

Jones started using augmented reality (AR) to make what looked like ordinary artwork come to life. This started bringing in a fanbase, as more of his paintings started to sell. By 2019, he was painting portraits of influential people, especially those involved in the crypto community.

Jones was approached by KnownOrigin to create NFTs on their platform. and the rest is history. From a struggling artist for years to being well known in just a few years is quite an origin story.

GxngYxng

This artist had been doing hand-drawn art for years since he was a child and getting in trouble for it at school. His name is pronounced *Gong Yang* and he had always wanted to be an animator, so he studied 3D and 2D animation and started work at an animation company to live that dream. He loved it because he could be creative but also didn't, because he wasn't working for himself.

In May 2021 GxngYxng submitted 100 pieces of art, called Ghxts, on OpenSea as an NFT collection. It got a lot of attention because it was different from what was on the platform. The collection was sold for .001 ETH each at the time and is now bringing in as much as 30 ETH and more with each resell in just 2 months.

GxngYxng has now expanded the collection to 1,000 pieces of work and has quit his day job.

Choosing a Marketplace Platform

It's very important to choose a platform that works best for you. Since there is a lot to choose from, I will list some of the easiest to use, but ultimately you need to research what's out there and choose the one with which you're most comfortable.

If you are already a digital artist that has a relatively good fanbase, then you should consider Nifty Gateway, Knoworigin, SuperRare, Rarible, or Foundation.

The first three are invite-only, but you could get invited to join as long as you've got a portfolio of your work and enough people supporting your work. There is an application process and you can get up-voted if these marketplaces want your work.

If you're just looking to trade, then Coinbase and eToro are good platforms for new traders.

Gas Fees

It isn't always free to create an NFT, as a lot of the marketplace platforms charge a gas fee to pay for the cost of creating the NFT on Ethereum's blockchain. Nifty Gateway charges 5% and an additional $0.30 for each secondary sale thereafter. Foundation is the most expensive and charges up to 15% if you want it done quickly against a busy network.

The fees change constantly, so it's always best to keep a good chunk of cryptocurrency in your virtual wallet to pay for these extra costs. Keep enough money aside for these fees for the creation of one NFT, unless you're planning on creating a lot more at once. You should be okay with $100 or so, but as the fees change all the time, have at least double that on hand.

Popular Marketplaces

There are numerous marketplace platforms with more springing up all time. A lot of the platforms have secondary marketplaces, and each platform can operate differently depending on what it's for and what the marketplace intends on achieving.

Nifty Gateway

This marketplace is owned by a very popular cryptocurrency exchange called Gemini. It works with popular artists, like the DJ Steve Aoki, Grimes, and 3LAU. It also has a secondary marketplace that allows collectors to resell artwork. In this marketplace, artists have the option to choose the percentages they want from these secondary sales.

You can either use ETH tokens or connect a credit card to use the website like an everyday online purchase. This makes it a lot easier to use because you don't need to have anything cryptocurrency-related to sign up and buy an item.

Limited-edition collections are created that are available for a specific period, called a *drop*.

There are different methods to purchase:

- Online silent auction: you can place a blind bid and wait to see if you won.

- Draw: very much a raffle or lottery, giving you an advantage based on the number of entries you place. It was also created as a detriment for bots getting top NFTs.

- Open edition: for a period of 5 to 15 minutes, an unlimited number of NFTs are available on a piece, making it a grab for all.

- Global offer: you can put in an offer that the owners get and can decide if they want to sell to you or not; this is available for anyone around the world.

To sell an NFT you upload it to your Nifty Gateway omnibus wallet using MetaMask. This is the only way you can do it. If you want to become a creator to sell, then you need to apply via an eight-part questionnaire on the website and then complete an interview.

AtomicMarket

Now, this is quite a unique marketplace platform as it is a shared liquidity NFT market smart contract. Shared liquidity means that everything listed on the one marketplace platform also shows in other marketplace platforms.

A smart contract is a program on the blockchain that performs actions depending on various conditions being met. An example of this is when a vehicle is registered; all the details are added by the user and the registration is done.

AtomicMarket is used by various websites to provide users with a unique and good experience. NFTs are given the name AtomicAssets and it's one of the few platforms that verify well-known collections. This means that you are guaranteed to be buying the genuine item. It's very strict with its collections and will blacklist any malicious collections it finds.

OpenSea

This is a peer-to-peer platform, so individuals interact directly with each other without third-party interference. It calls itself a purveyor of rare digital items and collectibles and only charges gas fees after the sale at 2.5%. When you create an account to browse the NFT collections it has, you can sort these by sales volume, should you wish to discover new artists.

It operates on Ethereum but users can sell in any currency and users can even add their own currency by contacting the company and asking for it to be listed. This platform also allows users to purchase, sell, and explore in virtual worlds, like Decentraland, Axis, and more.

SuperRare

This marketplace is more like a social network, but it also operates as a marketplace for the buying and selling of NFTs that are rare and original. The cryptocurrency used on it is Ethereum, so you need to purchase the currency ETH to make purchases on the platform. SuperRare charges 3% for purchases, a percentage the buyers must pay.

It is different because each piece of art that is featured is a single edition, so that raises its rarity value. It is constantly evolving to be more social and has updated the personalized notifications on its home page. These include an activity feed to keep its users updated with anything they should know.

It's a great platform for artists that are just starting out and have artwork that is innovative and creative.

BakerySwap

BakerySwap isn't just an NFT marketplace platform; it's a multifunctional crypto hub that offers a large number and range of decentralized financial services and a crypto launchpad.

A crypto launchpad is a place that provides ways to raise capital for new projects. It also allows investors to gain early access to these projects, as well as getting tokens at a reduced price before release. It's a very good way to entice investors. Crypto launchpads also vet new projects, so that investors are not at risk.

On the NFT side, BakerySwap has its own tokens, called BAKE, that are used when the platform is hosting digital art, meme competitions, and NFTs in games. It is said to be one of the easiest NFT platforms to mint and sell artwork.

Rarible

Rarible has a similar concept to OpenSea and is an open marketplace for artists and creators to issue and sell NFTs. In fact, Rarible allows you to view and manage your OpenSea collectibles on their platform.

It has its own token: the RARI. These are issued for users who wish to have a say on its platform with regards to things like fees and community rules. Users that wish to invest in the development of the platform purchase these tokens to be more actively involved and not just use it as a marketplace.

You can choose to not sell your NFT until you're ready, gift it to someone, or even have it destroyed completely using the platform.

Foundation

This is an exclusive community that doesn't let just anyone use their platform. For artists to gain entry, they must either receive an invitation from fellow creators on the platform or get up-votes. This just means that creators that are on the platform can suggest someone and the community votes on whether they can put their work on.

Once an artist is given the green light to join, they need to purchase gas to mint their NFTs. This means they need to pay in cryptocurrency the cost of creating that NFT, and prices do fluctuate.

All of these criteria ensure that this platform is very exclusive and has very good work on its platform, which ensures higher prices are paid by buyers.

Another exciting aspect of Foundation is that it isn't just about NFT creation, buying, and selling. It is also heavily involved in allowing artists to experiment and create things akin to hackathons, meaning creative people are brought together to create something new by experimenting with the technology.

Cargo

This marketplace is relatively unknown in the media but is a good platform for beginners. It also supports the ETH cryptocurrency, but anyone can create an account and mint their NFTs.

Its first unique feature is that there are no auctions; artists price their work and if anyone likes it, they can buy it.

The second feature that is unique about it is the ability to split royalties, so artists can collaborate and share in the royalties because up to 15 unique wallet addresses can be added to a single NFT.

There are no gas fees because it relies on a feature called 'magic minting' and is an easy platform to use.

Myth Market

Myth Market is actually an umbrella marketplace for four other marketplaces: GPK. Market, GoPepe.Market, KOGS.Market, and Shatner.Market. It's no wonder they call themselves a "series of convenient online marketplaces." This just means that these other marketplaces operate on this platform and you choose which one you want to use to trade.

The focus of this NFT marketplace platform is on trading cards only, and the only cryptocurrency that is supported is WAX. This stands for The Worldwide Asset eXchange and is both a type of blockchain technology as well as cryptocurrency. WAX coins can be bought at most crypto exchanges.

Mintable

On Mintable you will find anything that can be an NFT from art, music, game items, collectibles, and more. It too is based on the Ethereum blockchain but has a gasless minting option. MINT tokens are used for users to participate in the platform's DAO. This allows users to vote on any platform changes, and can be earned by the buying and selling of NFTs on the platform or can be purchased.

There are also three auction types to choose from: time, buy it now, and the traditional auction. Another unique feature is the integration it has with OpenSea, so any collections you have there can be managed on Mintable and vice versa, which is handy, especially for trading.

Creating an NFT

The steps to create an NFT will differ depending on which platform you choose. In the following example, we will use the Mintable marketplace platform because it is quite easy to use and a favorite for those starting out.

Create a MetaMask Wallet

This is a web3 cryptocurrency wallet, meaning a wallet with a chrome extension that lets you interact with the NFT marketplace platform of your choice.

MetaMask is the most popular one to use and is where all your digital currency will be held. Other wallets to consider are Formatic, Coinbase, Wallet, Torus, and Portis.

For most platforms, you will need to buy ETH first and have some in your wallet before creating an account. This is for the gas fees should the platform charge any.

Create an Account

Once you have chosen a marketplace platform from either the list I have given you or based on your own research, you need to sign up for an account, like you would do with any website. You will have the option in this step to allow access to your MetaMask wallet.

Minting the NFT

The steps I have highlighted are subject to change and may differ from other marketplace platforms.

1. On the top of the Mintable webpage, you will see 'Mint an Item.' Select that.

2. Select "Create a new item."

3. Choose either traditional or gasless, depending on whether you want to pay any exorbitant charges. For this example, we are going with the traditional option.

4. Choose the type of item you want to make into an NFT. Your options are art, collectibles, game items, music, domains, templates, or videos. We'll use the collectible option.

5. You will see a box that you can tick, should you wish to, next to the words Mint in the Mintable Store. This just means that if you click in the box, whatever you turn into an NFT will be part of Mintable's collection and most platforms offer this option. It's the most cost-effective option because you are not paying to host your digital item anywhere. The only time you wouldn't select this option is when you are relatively well known and want to keep your work under your label or brand. Once the option is selected, the token address for the item is

provided, which is your smart contract for the item. The token ID is also provided at this stage.

6. Select "Only mint my token" unless you have a lot of items that you want to mint.

7. Create a Token Name, listing title, and listing subtitle.

8. Now you come across an option to upload a private/unlockable item. This is where you can embed various items into your NFT that only the owner can access. This can be a great option for making your NFT unique.

9. Now you can upload the image you want to mint into an NFT.

10. The last step is to add "other metadata," like the name of the data and value. But it isn't needed to complete the minting, so you can skip this step if you wish to do so.

11. Once you click on "List this item," a pop-up screen appears telling you that you are about to make a blockchain transaction.

12. Either you cancel to continue adding information or click "proceed."

13. Your MetaMask wallet will then automatically open up. It will show you what the total gas charges will be for this NFT creation.

14. If you have enough ETH, you can click on "confirm"; otherwise, you need to add some Ether to your wallet first.

15. Once you click "confirm," a pop-up screen appears, confirming that you have minted an NFT.

16. You can click to view the item from this screen or just go to your profile and view it from there.

Putting the NFT up for Sale

Once the NFT is minted and showing on your profile, you can put it up for sale or transfer. If you want it to be available for sale, then follow these steps:

1. You need to give it a category, listing title, subtitle, and description.

2. The important checkbox is "Transfer copyright when purchased." That means the owner can use the item commercially without repercussions. If you have a reason to not allow copyright movement, then this is where you specify.

3. Then you can choose the option for the buyer to resell. You don't really want to uncheck this box because you should allow the trade to occur.

4. You need to also choose a fixed price in US dollars that will show the ETH amount below it.

5. Then click "List this item" and your MetaMask wallet will open up again. It will have its own pop-up screen asking you to sign the transaction or cancel.

6. Choose "sign" and proceed.

7. You get a pop-up screen again to confirm the transaction.

And now your NFT is ready to be sold on Mintable.

The NFT's After-Sale Journey

Once your artwork is sold and if you didn't pass on the copyright, this is what happens:

- You as the artist own the copyright and the buyer receives a certificate of ownership. This data will change as the piece is bought and sold, tracking each owner in the blockchain.

- If you as the artist selected any secondary sale fees, then these apply here so with each resell you will gain a royalty payment.

Chapter 7:

NFT Trading

There are a lot of NFT Marketplace platforms that allow you to buy and sell NFTs by bidding, and some even allow you to get free NFTs. Marketplaces that are like cryptocurrency exchanges are beneficial to purchase from because of the high resale value you might find here.

NFTs that are in high demand can have a high resale value immediately after they are released, but you can't determine that unless you use this type of marketplace. The reason is that here you will be able to compare previous sales to gauge demand for resale.

In this chapter, I will take you through the different marketplaces that sell the best NFTs per type and then describe a couple to choose from for resale. This way you can navigate through the different types to start trading.

Buying Specific NFTs

Before you can start trading, there are questions that you need to first consider.

What NFT marketplace platform should I use to buy NFTs?

Since there is a range of NFTs to invest in, I have listed where you can buy NFTs for different items that are good for trading and then specific ones for art trading options.

What cryptocurrency is needed to buy these NFTs?

Most run off Ethereum so the currency is ETH. Some allow for other currencies as well, and there are a couple that allow you to buy with your credit card. You need to check each platform's FAQ page, as this changes as improvements are made on the platforms.

Are the NFTs available in a limited drop?

Drops are limited sales; artists will sell a collection or a piece of artwork at a specific price for a specified time on that marketplace.

For trading, these types of sales can be beneficial because only rare items get sold this way, so you want to buy when these drops happen. Make sure you don't just buy something at a high price and expect a high return though. See what items are trending and stick to those, but don't spend too much.

Below are specific items that yield high trades and the marketplaces that you should look at using for such items.

Basketball

NBA Top Shot was created for licensed collectibles and deals with digital, collectible basketball cards that are far more interactive than normal trading cards. They contain in-game highlights for each featured player. The highest selling card was the one for Lebron James that featured a clip of him dunking on the Houston Rockets. It was called the *Lebron James Dunk* card and sold for $200,000 (Conti, 2021).

This marketplace is extremely popular now, and if you're a basketball fan then it won't take much research to know digital cards are trending. Even if you are not a basketball fan, you will be able to find out what the top teams are and who are the best players to see which cards will bring you the most profit.

Video Games

Online video games have been gaining popularity over the years, to the point that one can earn a substantial living just by playing video games. With Axie Infinity, professional gaming has truly reached another level entirely. On this NFT marketplace, you can raise, trade, and battle 'Axies,' which are digital pets. Think of Pokémon but online.

In-game tokens, called AXS, are used to trade when performing any action, which in turn can be traded for ETH and then swapped for the traditional currency. The number of active players around the world is sitting at 90,000 and growing with its popularity. This is why the most expensive Axie pet was sold for $788,000 (Ong, 2021).

Virtual real estate is also being sold here because tokens can also be earned by building kingdoms for these pets. The main trading opportunity comes with just playing the game and getting involved in the community. There is money to be made on this platform but it doesn't work like other marketplaces.

Virtual Real Estate

I spoke about virtual worlds in Chapter 4 and gave you some information on Decentraland. The buying and selling of virtual real estate is incredibly popular, especially if said virtual real estate is located in Decentraland. This destination is the place to be, with digital artists buying real estate to display their art in virtual galleries. Even Sotheby's has an art gallery there.

It does cost thousands of dollars to buy a parcel of land but it is worth the price. The more parcels bought, the more that can be done with the land, which includes renting out the space.

So, just like physical real estate, virtual real estate is a great investment option. It can be a little more involved than other NFTs though, so your best option is to work with a company called Public Realm that was created especially for digital real estate investing.

Despite the complexity involved, it is well worth the effort, and the time is now to get in there and start buying!

Soccer

Sorare is based on the fantasy football premise; users can collect player cards to play in weekly fantasy matches. The platform works with Ethereum and has licensed player information with over 140 soccer (European football) clubs from the United States, Europe, and Asia.

Cards contain player statistics and rarity with the most expensive card being sold for $102,000. The card was of Cristiano Ronaldo, and with over two billion soccer fans worldwide it is a very popular trading site.

Music

A platform called BAND Royalty is well ahead of the market and allows fans to get NFTs and then stake them to earn royalties. Instead of earning money via NFT trading, you could earn quite a good passive income this way. You just need to create an account to purchase this type of NFT and have ETH in your MetaMask wallet. You then join the Music Mogul Club by buying one BAND NFT and start staking!

This is how staking works: Stakes get an additional 5% of OpenSea Ethereum trades, so a discount as it were. The NFTs are staked in the BAND Royalty pools, which decreases the supply in tradable markets. This increases the value of the NFT so you gain more.

There are also three music pools that fans or users can choose from: publishing, mechanical or public performance, and interest. Stakers can stake from 91 days to 5 years. The longer the stake, the higher the earning.

BAND Royalty receives the royalties directly from the music industry leaders and then shares this at 50% with the stakers. Revenue is earned when the artists play and their work is streamed and published in the music collection held on the BAND Royalty's platform.

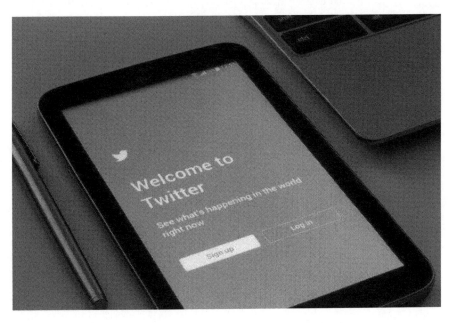

Tweets

Ever since the first-ever tweet was sold for $2.9 million, tweets are now the thing to collect. Valuables is the only NFT marketplace that sells tweets. As long as you have ETH, you can create an account, then copy and paste the URL of the tweet you want to buy in the search bar.

The platform will inform the sender of the tweet that someone wants to buy it, and then the transaction takes place. But if it's a very popular tweet then there will be bidding taking place. The owner of the tweet gets to decide on who wins. The winner receives a minted NFT containing the owner's signature.

Anyone can use the platform and tweets range from rare to everyday tweets. It's gaining in popularity, especially as pretty much everyone is on Twitter, so owning a celebrity tweet can be profitable. It is akin to having that person's autograph in this digital age.

This is a great place to trade if you are on your Twitter account daily, so know what is trending to put in an offer.

There are three snags at the moment:

1. If the creator hasn't accepted your offer to buy, you are still charged the gas fees.

2. You do not own the copyright.

3. Even though you can resell the tweet, you need to use OpenSea for this at the moment.

NFT Art Trading

If you have some capital to get into NFT art trading then at the moment you are guaranteed some good returns. You do need quite a bit of money first, like physical art investing, but you don't have to be a millionaire to get started. You just need enough to buy cryptocurrency for gas fees and to buy the art itself.

It's difficult to provide you with an estimate of how much you need to get started because gas fees change quite often, and the same goes for buying digital art to sell. You would need to look at what you have to spend and then calculate from there. Never start with credit and always watch the market for trends.

A good tip is to follow artists and crypto investors on social media pages, like Twitter and Instagram, because they are more likely to know what niche is getting popular. Twitter is the most used, so create an account if you don't have one already, and start following investors and artists talking about NFTs.

The key is to get in when this is starting to trend, so that you can buy cheaply and sell as the prices rise. Also, look at what kind of artwork is already out there, including what these were being bought for a few months ago and what their value is now. That should indicate to you that that particular niche is now saturated.

If you do have a nice amount of capital to get some high-end pieces, then trade on Nifty Gateway, OpenSea, SuperRare, Rarible, and Foundation. These marketplaces started it all and continue to keep rare pieces that go for a lot of money.

They also do drops regularly, so if you are keeping an eye on trends and emerging artists, you can get a collection of theirs at one of these drops quite cheaply and then sell each piece at a good rate.

You also want to have more than one marketplace account, so that you can diversify. Generally, popular artists will be selling their work at very high prices, but you will find drops being done by them as well. These are great buys because you could get a collection of a famous artist for a few hundred dollars and sell each piece back at a high price, because the artist is popular.

Don't purchase art from a secondary market because that is a risk and could cost you a lot of money, with no guarantee of a return investment.

Even though crypto art trading could result in a lot of money made, there are so many types of NFTs out there with more being created that you should consider investing in these as well.

Chapter 8:

The Step-by-Step Guide to Creating NFTs and Making a Profit

With all the information provided, I thought it was best to recap by laying out a very simple step-by-step guide as a checklist for you to follow.

Creating an NFT to Sell

1. Create a piece of digital art or scan a piece of physical art in high definition.

2. Create a MetaMask wallet.

3. Buy ETH.

4. Choose an NFT marketplace platform.

5. Create an account with that platform.

6. Create an NFT by following the steps that the platform provides.

7. Pay the gas fees.

8. Put the NFT up for sale.

9. Promote your art of social media or via friends and family.

Buying NFTs to Sell

1. Create a MetaMask wallet.

2. Add ETH.

3. Choose a couple of high-end NFT marketplace platforms.

4. Create multiple accounts and subscribe to their mailing lists to be notified of drops.

5. Watch Twitter for trends and niches gaining interest.

6. Based on that information, buy NFTs that are selling cheaply in drops that are part of a collection.

7. Sell each piece from that collection on a secondary marketplace within an hour of purchase.

If you stick to these steps, you will start seeing profits.

Hints and Tips

What follows are a few things to look out for on your journey to NFT trading. It's important to bear these in mind and follow them so that you get the most out of this experience.

Trends

The key is to always be on the lookout for trends and to purchase when prices are low. Twitter is the best source, but as you look to expand your trading then join Discord discussions on emerging technology and topics to gain better insight.

Most platforms have a link in their FAQs that you can use to sign up and join Discord. It is an online communication platform that is quite popular for discussions.

Secondary Marketplaces

Never purchase from a secondary marketplace because you will pay more for NFTs and there is a low chance that you will be able to resell for a profit. Those marketplaces are where people mostly buy to collect, so you want to only sell on the secondary market

Gas Fees

Always be wary of gas fees and have enough ETH to cover these. Make it part of your buying budget, so that it isn't a surprise after each mint or purchase.

Patience

Even though NFT trading is a hot topic and a lot of people have made money, it is something that might take a little time. Follow the steps listed at the beginning of the chapter and keep at it. The trick is to buy and sell at the right moment, and only with time will you learn what to look out for.

Chapter 9:

Investing Risks and Scams

Even though NFTs and the marketplace platforms are minted and created on the blockchain, you still need to be aware of the risks.

How to Stay Safe and Secure

Using something digitally and being online doesn't mean it's safe from a security perspective. So it's important to keep yourself safe and secure at all times.

This chapter isn't here to scare you and shun the internet, but merely to guide you on best practices.

Internet Safety

It is essential to have good antivirus software before browsing the internet. There are numerous options to choose from, based on your price range. Please don't use any that are free because they will not provide you with adequate security.

Among the best ones available are: Bitdefender, Kaspersky, Webroot, Norton, Trend Micro, McAfee, ESET, and Avast.

Multifactor Authentication

This method is used to protect you from being hacked when you are logging onto websites. To access these sites, you need to provide two or more pieces of information to verify that it is you. This is incredibly important and you can download an app on your phone to set this up. You can choose from these five that are considered the best on the market: Authy, Google Authenticator, andOTP, LastPass Authenticator, and Microsoft Authenticator.

In March 2021, several users on Nifty Gateway failed to use multifactor authentication and had collections taken from their wallets, as well as more purchases made using the cryptocurrency in their virtual wallets. The company wasn't hacked; the users just didn't have the right security in place to safeguard their accounts.

Scams to Watch Out For

There are some things to be aware of when doing NFT trading so that you don't fall for a scam. NFTs are new technology and very popular, so it would make sense that the criminal element sees this as a great opportunity to prey on those who are not secure and don't know what to look out for. As part of looking for trends to buy and sell NFTs, keep a lookout for precautions and new developments, so that you can keep safe.

NFT Storage

Not everyone follows best practices and some sellers store their NFTs on centralized servers. This could mean that the NFT could vanish if that server is damaged or destroyed. That's why it's important to verify storage when purchasing, to ensure that your NFT will keep existing. This applies to NFTs you are collecting or holding onto to sell later.

Fake NFTs

A lot of marketplaces may list work that isn't the artist's work, so it is up to you to do the extra research to ensure you have the correct NFT and that it is being sold with the artist's permission.

You can perform a reverse-image search to see if it appears on more marketplaces but is named differently. Artists can list their work in more than one place, but it is not possible for them to name it differently.

For example, two of the biggest marketplaces, OpenSea and Rarible, don't require owner verification, so as a buyer you need to be aware of this.

Phishing Sites

With the creation of so many NFT marketplace platforms and more popping up daily, it's important to note that not all are safe.

Phishing sites do exist. These mimic being authentic NFT marketplaces and steal user log-in credentials to steal collections for trade. These will look like legitimate marketplaces, so do your research before creating an account. Giveaways are misspelled words on the website like 'cryptocurrency' being spelt as 'cryptokurrency,' so keep a lookout for these.

This is also where your multifactor authentication app comes in, to shield you from losing your information and collection.

Fake Support

Because of the need for more information around NFTs, scammers have created customer support channels and social media accounts offering more information.

Be wary of any place asking you for personal information because they use that to get access to your account. Getting information is one thing, exchanging that for information about yourself is a red flag.

Giveaways

Also don't click on any strange links. There are no free giveaways or drops that require you to click on a link. If you see any strange emails that, for example, come from a site you know to be reputable, don't click on it. Instead, just go directly to the site on your browser. If the email is legitimate, the same information can be found on the site directly. The same goes for seeing any pop-up giveaways on social media.

Drops can go for very little money but never for free, so that should be a huge clue that you're seeing a scam.

Wash Trading

There have been cases whereby NFT owners have inflated the price by creating fake hype. They are known as 'crypto whales' because they hold a large amount of cryptocurrency in their virtual wallets. They then sell an NFT from one wallet to another at a higher price than it's worth. Because the scammer owns both wallets, this is known as 'wash trading.'

Fake Virtual Wallet Apps

A user had downloaded what he thought to be a virtual wallet named after the Trezor wallet. He lost all his cryptocurrency and was not pleased that the Apple store had a fraudulent app.

The reality is that it is easy to create apps that pass most security checks. That is why internet security is very important. If the user took the time to double-check the app in comparison to what the real thing looks like, he would still have a full virtual wallet.

Stick to known apps and virtual wallets and always double-check the spelling, as well as the look of the app.

Chapter 10:

The Pros and Cons of NFTs

Since the information is vast, I thought it might be helpful to include a section on pros and cons so you have one handy when deciding to start trading. This is by no means a way to prevent you from wanting to take advantage of the biggest thing in cryptocurrency to date. This is merely to ensure that you are fully equipped and well informed before you start trading. It is a final check, as it were, to reinforce the reasons for wanting to be part of something exciting and very profitable, and also part of technological history.

Cons

Unpredictability

Prices are high for collectibles and don't hold value in the long term so it is a gamble due to the unpredictable nature of this type of trade. This is happening because it is so new and exciting, so everyone wants to be a part of it, especially investors.

This is pushing up prices, but even though NFTs can sell for a lot of money, the prices have come down. It is not always a guarantee to make millions on a piece.

The same can be said about any artwork that is new and exciting: everyone rushes in to be part of it and the popularity makes it expensive. But it is by no means a bubble that will burst, just the start of the technological revolution and a new way to make money smartly and without a lot of hard labor involved.

Security

If details are entered incorrectly or passwords are not kept safe then NFTs can be stolen or lost. Many artists have had their work tokenized without their knowledge, and it isn't clear how one can reclaim ownership at this stage. However, the same can be said about forgeries in the art world. There are also cases of art provenance being corrupted, which again can impact on the validity of a piece of art's history.

The safest way is to adhere to the same rules for any internet transaction as this is an issue with other online payments as well. It is not a new type of security issue; it is only highlighted because every person needs to ensure they follow the protocols needed to keep their information safe and secure so that they can use the internet safely.

Pros

Artist Benefit

Artists can collect royalties and be paid for their work that can't be copied, so it guarantees that artists are taken care of and knockoffs are not being found everywhere. As an NFT artist, not only is this a good way to ensure your artwork is seen, but to also continuously earn from each resale. It's making it easier to live that passionate dream and make a living off of it.

Bringing Art to Everyone

Collectables and art are more interactive and engaging, with a variety to look at and enjoy. NFTs are making art collection and appreciation something everyone can experience. It's like an art and collectibles revival, with so many options and new technology that it is exciting. It's just what the world needs now and going forward, and hopefully it is here to stay.

Authenticity

Ownership is added to the ledger and verified against the item, so you are guaranteed an authentic item that increases in value. Blockchain technology is integrated into how NFTs are created and used, so transactions are put on a ledger and tracked. Ownership is tracked with each sale.

Ease

NFTs are easy to create and sell, as there are so many marketplaces to choose from, with a range of features and handy step-by-step instructions to follow. This makes buying and selling crypto digital art straightforward.

Passive Income

Finally, trading NFTs are a great way to bring in passive income. If you're a digital artist, you do need to create something first to mint into an NFT but the return investment is enough for you not to need to sell a piece every day or week.

By just trading in NFTs, many people are earning thousands if not millions by buying the right piece cheaply, just as it is about to trend, and then selling it for a higher price. It just comes down to keeping an eye on the market for the right trends.

Conclusion

I hope that my book was able to help you gain insight into the NFT process, as well as how you can get started in trading NFTs. It is a good passive income source, but also one that takes planning, with the correct information to make the right decisions.

With so many marketplaces to choose from for the different types of trade available, anything can be bought and sold as an NFT as long as you have some cryptocurrency to start off with in your virtual wallet!

Start now, create your virtual wallet, buy ETH, and use Mintable by following the steps provided to get a feel for the layout. Very soon you will be trading like a pro and earning profits on new and emerging NFTs or rare collectibles.

If you're a digital artist, you could see yourself getting the recognition you deserve and your art will bring in enough money so you might finally be able to quit your day job and keep creating!

Finally, please know that I am not a financial advisor and cannot give out financial advice. I am providing information based on my research only.

I hope that the information has been insightful and gives you confidence that this is the future of trading and that you are part of history in the making.

Good luck with your endeavors!

References

3D Gladiator. (2021, March 5). How to turn PHYSICAL artworks into NFTs! [Video]. Youtube. https://www.youtube.com/watch?v=99wzZFrPJxc

Adam Back. (2021, June 6). Wikipedia. https://en.wikipedia.org/wiki/Adam_Back

AOPA's Pilot Information Center. (2016, August 18). Fractional ownership: Overview. AOPA Foundation. https://www.aopa.org/pic-archive/aircraft-ownership/fractional-ownership-overview

Aparaschivei, L. (2021, March 21). How to create NFTs. Vectornator. https://www.vectornator.io/blog/how-to-create-nfts

Axie Infinity. (2021, July 20). Wikipedia. https://en.wikipedia.org/wiki/Axie_Infinity

Babbar, S. (2021, June 24). NFTs: Fad or breakthrough? In the Black. https://www.intheblack.com/articles/2021/06/24/nfts-fad-or-breakthrough

Binance Academy. (2021, May 5). What is Decentraland (MANA)? Binance Academy. https://academy.binance.com/en/articles/what-is-decentraland

Blog Herald. (2020, August 13). Content creation platforms that pay in crypto. The Blog Herald. https://blogherald.com/general/content-creation-platforms-that-pay-in-crypto/

Bruzenak, J. H. (2015, July). Fractional ownership—Time-share RVing. Retire to an RV. http://www.retiretoanrv.com/rv-retirement-basics/newbees-getting-started/what-rv-do-i-choose/fractional-ownership-time-share-rving/

Buchanan, T. (2016, May 25). How Hollywood has predicted VR in movies. VRScout. https://vrscout.com/news/how-hollywood-predicted-vr-in-movies/

Cardinal, D. (2021, July 1). How you can still make money mining cryptocurrency. Extremetech. https://www.extremetech.com/extreme/323876-how-you-can-still-make-money-mining-cryptocurrency

Cascone, S. (2021, June 21). Here are the 14 most expensive NFTs sold to date, from Beeple to Mad Dog Jones and beyond. Artnet News. https://news.artnet.com/market/updated-most-expensive-nfts-1980942

Chen, J. (2020, December 28). Speculation definition. Investopedia. https://www.investopedia.com/terms/s/speculation.asp

Chow, A. (2021, March 22). NFTs are shaking up the art world—But they could change so much more. Time. https://time.com/5947720/nft-art/

Clark, M. (2021, March 11). People are spending millions on NFTs. What? Why? The Verge. https://www.theverge.com/22310188/nft-explainer-what-is-blockchain-crypto-art-faq

Clavien, A. (2020, September 2). Is fractional ownership a sustainable investment option? London Trade Art Magazine. https://www.londontradeart.co.uk/en/magazine/is-fractional-ownership-a-sustainable-investment-option

Conti, R. (2021, April 29). What you need to know about non-fungible tokens (NFTs). Forbes Advisor.

https://www.forbes.com/advisor/investing/nft-non-fungible-token/

Conway, L. (2020, February 1). Blockchain, explained. Investopedia. https://www.investopedia.com/terms/b/blockchain.asp

Coppola, G. (2018, September 16). Porsche targets Uber-loving millennials with luxury car rentals. Independent OnLine. https://www.iol.co.za/business-report/companies/porsche-targets-uber-loving-millennials-with-luxury-car-rentals-17050917

Corporate Trash. (2021, July 29). The rise of Ghxsts: How NFT artist GxngYxng built a 1-of-1 community. MomentRanks. https://momentranks.com/blog/the-rise-of-ghxsts-how-nft-artist-gxngyxng-built-a-1-of-1-community

Costello, A. (2020, February 21). The history of first cryptocurrencies before Bitcoin. Medium. https://medium.com/hashmart-blog/the-history-of-first-cryptocurrencies-before-Bitcoin-6eccebca152a

CryptoKing. (2021, May 6). NFTs about to get a whole lot saucier! CoinTribune. https://www.cointribune.com/en/columns/the-nft-column/nfts-about-to-get-a-whole-lot-saucier/

CryptoPunks. (2021, February 26). Wikipedia. https://en.wikipedia.org/wiki/CryptoPunks

Curvy Road. (n.d.). Curvy Road, an exotic car share company offering fractional ownership and time share of exotic sports cars & high-end luxury automobiles Bentley, Ferrari, Lamborghini. Retrieved July 21, 2021, https://www.curvyroad.com/aboutcurvyroad.php

Daniels, C. (2021, March 2). Where did NFT's come from? The history of non-fungible tokens [Video]. Youtube. https://www.youtube.com/watch?v=uJnzykET3aQ

Dazn Newsdesk. (2021, May 8). What are NFTs? How do I buy them? How can I sell them? DAZN. https://www.dazn.com/en-US/news/boxing/what-are-nfts-how-do-i-buy-them-how-can-i-sell-them/6lzungqnrak01lbd4pu4c6oc9

de la Garza, A. (2021, March 18). Digital NFT art is booming—But at what cost? Time. https://time.com/5947911/nft-environmental-toll/

Dean & Associates. (n.d.). Short history of fractional ownership. Dean & Associates. Retrieved July 18, 2021, http://dean-and-associates.com/blog/short-history-of-fractional-ownership-1

del Castillo, M. (n.d.). Blockchain 50. Forbes. Retrieved July 16, 2021, https://www.forbes.com/sites/michaeldelcastillo/2020/02/19/blockchain-50/?sh=7c2d02067553

Diablo, D. (2021, April 6). Don Diablo presents DESTINATION HEXAGONIA [Video]. Youtube. https://www.youtube.com/watch?v=XOqH6Fs43XE

Discover Boating. (n.d.). Fractional boat ownership 101. Discover Boating. Retrieved July 18, 2021, https://www.discoverboating.com/resources/fractional-boat-ownership

Don Diablo. (2021, May 26). Wikipedia. https://en.wikipedia.org/wiki/Don_Diablo

Dredge, S. (2016, November 10). The complete guide to virtual reality—Everything you need to get started. The Guardian. https://www.theguardian.com/technology/2016/nov/10/virtual-reality-guide-headsets-apps-games-vr

Duetzmann, S. (2020, October 2). Video game definition of the week: "Skins." Engaged Family Gaming. https://engagedfamilygaming.com/videogames/video-game-definition-of-the-week-skins/

E-gold. (2020, July 4). Wikipedia. https://en.wikipedia.org/wiki/E-gold

Engle, J. (2017, July 30). How I digitize my art [Video]. Youtube. https://www.youtube.com/watch?v=w2zzEeC247k

ET Online. (2017, October 25). 5 reasons why you should go for cryptocurrency. The Economic Times. https://economictimes.indiatimes.com/industry/banking/fina nce/5-reasons-why-you-should-go-for-cryptocurrency/articleshow/61184608.cms?from=mdr

Ethereum. (n.d.). Non-fungible tokens (NFT). Ethereum.org. https://Ethereum.org/en/nft/

Everydays: The First 5000 Days. (2021, June 5). Wikipedia. https://en.wikipedia.org/wiki/Everydays:_the_First_5000_Da ys

Fractional ownership. (2021, June 15). Wikipedia. https://en.wikipedia.org/wiki/Fractional_ownership

Fractional ownership of property. (2007, September 8). Privateproperty. https://www.privateproperty.co.za/advice/property/articles/fr actional-ownership-of-property/912

Frank, R. (2021, March 30). Crypto investor who bought Beeple's NFT for $69 million says he would have paid even more. CNBC. https://www.cnbc.com/2021/03/30/vignesh-sundaresan-known-as-metakovan-on-paying-69-million-for-beeple-nft.html

Frankenfield, J. (2021, July 13). Off-chain transactions (cryptocurrency) definition. Investopedia. https://www.investopedia.com/terms/o/offchain-transactions-cryptocurrency.asp

Gina. (2020, June 1). In-game collectibles: The evolution of a tedious task. CBR. https://www.cbr.com/video-game-collectibles-evolution/

Greenwood, M. (2018, August 15). How to digitize original artwork [Video]. Youtube. https://www.youtube.com/watch?v=tUjsBokto_Q

Harper, J. (2021, March 23). Jack Dorsey's first ever tweet sells for $2.9m. BBC News. https://www.bbc.com/news/business-56492358

Hashcash. (2019, December 12). Wikipedia. https://en.wikipedia.org/wiki/Hashcash

Hernandez, B. (2021, July 13). The rise of NFT domains. Business 2 Community. https://www.business2community.com/business-innovation/the-rise-of-nft-domains-02418586

Houston, B. (n.d.). Virtual products & NFTs in the Metaverse. Threekit. Retrieved July 22, 2021, https://www.threekit.com/how-to-sell-virtual-products

How the laws & regulations affecting blockchain technology and cryptocurrencies, like Bitcoin, can impact its adoption. (2021, January 27). Business Insider. https://www.businessinsider.com/blockchain-cryptocurrency-regulations-us-global?IR=T

How to become a crypto artist. (2021, May 18). Art Rights https://www.artrights.me/en/profession-crypto-artist/

IBM. (n.d.). What is blockchain technology? https://www.ibm.com/topics/what-is-blockchain

Internet meme. (2018, December 1). Wikipedia https://en.wikipedia.org/wiki/Internet_meme

Iredale, G. (2021, June 14). NFT marketplace: Everything you need to know. 101 Blockchains. https://101blockchains.com/nft-marketplace/

Ismail, K. (2021, January 21). The current state of blockchain. CMSWire.com. https://www.cmswire.com/information-management/a-look-at-the-current-state-of-blockchain/

Jones, E. T., & Bowden, J. (2021, April 26). NFTs are much bigger than an art fad—Here's how they could change the world. The Conversation. https://theconversation.com/nfts-are-much-bigger-than-an-art-fad-heres-how-they-could-change-the-world-159563

Kale, S. (2021, June 23). NFTs and me: Meet the people trying to sell their memes for millions. The Guardian. https://www.theguardian.com/technology/2021/jun/23/nfts-and-me-meet-the-people-trying-to-sell-their-memes-for-millions

Kay, G. (2021, March 20). We talked to crypto-art investors to figure out what's driving people to spend millions on NFTs, despite no guarantee their value will increase. Business Insider. https://www.businessinsider.com/why-are-people-buying-nfts-investing-in-nft-crypto-art-2021-3?IR=T

Khan, M. (2021, March 28). How to sell your article as an NFT. Medium. https://medium.com/swlh/how-to-sell-your-article-as-an-nft-a904690331fb

Klein, J. (2021, April 26). "A crazy success story": Trevor Jones' NFT gamble pays off. CoinDesk. https://www.coindesk.com/a-crazy-success-story-trevor-jones-nft-gamble-pays-off

Landi, H. (2020, February 6). How Anthem is using blockchain technology to free up members' data. FierceHealthcare. https://www.fiercehealthcare.com/tech/how-anthem-using-blockchain-technology-to-free-up-patients-data

Laszlo. (2021, May 14). What is a non-fungible token? Understanding the different types of NFTs. Medium. https://blog.indorse.io/what-is-a-non-fungible-token-understanding-the-different-types-of-nfts-3ef29a2b2876

Lennon, H. (2021, January 19). The false narrative of Bitcoin's role in illicit activity. Forbes. https://www.forbes.com/sites/haileylennon/2021/01/19/the-false-narrative-of-Bitcoins-role-in-illicit-activity/?sh=68f217933432

Lielacher, A. (2021a, January 5). 10 awesome uses of cryptocurrency. https://bravenewcoin.com/insights/10-awesome-uses-of-cryptocurrency

Lielacher, A. (2021b, May 26). How to become a crypto artist and earn an income by selling NFTs. Trust Wallet. https://trustwallet.com/blog/how-to-become-a-crypto-artist-and-earn

Liscia, V. D. (2021, June 10). First ever NFT sells for $1.4 million. Hyperallergic. https://hyperallergic.com/652671/kevin-mccoy-quantum-first-nft-created-sells-at-sothebys-for-over-one-million/

Luno. (2021, May 3). Top 10 most valuable NFTs ever sold. Luno. https://www.luno.com/blog/en/post/top-10-most-valuable-nfts-ever-sold

Malinga, S. (2021, June 24). SA money-lender now accepts NFTs as collateral. ITWeb. https://www.itweb.co.za/content/raYAyModAbRqJ38N

Malwa, S. (2021, February 9). Biggest ever NFT sale made as "Axie Land" goes for $1.5 million. Decrypt. https://decrypt.co/57092/biggest-ever-nft-sale-made-as-single-axie-land-goes-for-1-5-million

Manhattan District Attorney's Office. (n.d.). NFT scams and frauds. Manhattan District Attorney's Office. Retrieved August 3, 2021, https://www.manhattanda.org/nft-scams-and-frauds/

Market Business News. (n.d.). What is a speculative investment? Definition and meaning. Market Business News. Retrieved July 20, 2021, from https://marketbusinessnews.com/financial-glossary/speculative-investment/

McNamara, R. (2021, June 28). How to buy NFTs right now. Benzinga. https://www.benzinga.com/money/how-to-buy-nfts/

Metaverse. (2020, July 24). Wikipedia. https://en.wikipedia.org/wiki/Metaverse

Mintable. (2021). Questions on Opensea.io. Mintable. https://docs.mintable.app/Ethereum-version/faq/questions-on-opensea-matters

MOBI. (n.d.). About MOBI. MOBI. Retrieved July 26, 2021, https://dlt.mobi/about/

Motor Home Travel. (n.d.). Fractional ownership. Motor Home Travel. https://www.motorhometravel.com/fractional-ownership/

Myth Market review. (2021). Cryptowisser. Retrieved August 1, 2021, from https://www.cryptowisser.com/nft-marketplace/myth-market/

NetJets. (2021, July 10). Wikipedia. https://en.wikipedia.org/wiki/NetJets

Newberry, E. (2021, May 22). Should you (or anyone) buy NFTs? The Motley Fool. https://www.fool.com/the-ascent/buying-stocks/articles/should-you-or-anyone-buy-nfts/

NFTs Explained. (2021, May 10). The History and Origin of NFTs [Video]. Youtube. https://www.youtube.com/watch?v=AYkmsFvYIIY

Nick Szabo. (2019, September 24). Wikipedia. https://en.wikipedia.org/wiki/Nick_Szabo

Nigam, V. (2018, December 27). There is an existence of cryptocurrency before Bitcoin !! LinkedIn. https://www.linkedin.com/pulse/existence-cryptocurrency-before-Bitcoin-nigam-the-blockchain-guy-

Non-fungible token. (2021, March 13). Wikipedia. https://en.wikipedia.org/wiki/Non-fungible_token

Norris, W. (2021, March 15). Earn easy money mining Ethereum. Medium. https://levelup.gitconnected.com/earn-easy-money-mining-Ethereum-31dea7c1ed60

Oculus Quest 2. (2020, November 6). Wikipedia. https://en.wikipedia.org/wiki/Oculus_Quest_2

Oculus Rift. (2019, October 1). Wikipedia. https://en.wikipedia.org/wiki/Oculus_Rift

Ong, J. Y. (2021, June 25). The 6 best NFT marketplaces for buying all kinds of digital assets. Make Use Of. https://www.makeuseof.com/best-nft-marketplaces-buying-all-kinds-digital-assets/

OpenSea. (n.d.). Gunky's uprising. OpenSea. Retrieved July 20, 2021, https://opensea.io/assets/0xc92ca2b5b8a996ad2a6fdd97c6d7ed038e61c725/14500040043

OpenSea. (2020, November 25). 7 reasons to sell your NFTs on OpenSea. OpenSea Blog. https://opensea.io/blog/guides/7-reasons-to-sell-your-nfts-on-opensea/

Parisi, D. (2021, July 6). Fashion's obsession with NFTs grows as new marketplaces pop up. Glossy. https://www.glossy.co/fashion/fashions-obsession-with-nfts-grows-as-new-marketplaces-pop-up/

Pillsbury. (2021, May 28). How crypto and NFTs could help regular people become real estate tycoons. Pillsbury Law. https://www.pillsburylaw.com/en/news-and-insights/crypto-nfts-real-estate-tycoons.html

Pinnacle Advisory Group. (2014, July 23). The difference between saving, investing, and speculating [Video]. Youtube. https://www.youtube.com/watch?v=blnbxbftme0

Proof of work. (2021, June 25). Wikipedia. https://en.wikipedia.org/wiki/Proof_of_work

Propy. (n.d.). The first real estate NFT launched by Propy. Propy. Retrieved July 22, 2021, https://propy.com/browse/propy-nft/

Propy auctions world's first real estate NFT with ownership transfer. (2021, May 25). Businesswire. https://www.businesswire.com/news/home/20210525005839/en/Propy-Auctions-World%E2%80%99s-First-Real-Estate-NFT-with-Ownership-Transfer

Rarible. (n.d.). Notion—The all-in-one workspace for your notes, tasks, wikis, and databases. Notion. Retrieved July 31, 2021, https://www.notion.so/rarible/rarible-com-FAQ-a47b276aa1994f7c8e3bc96d700717c5

Reiff, N. (2021, May 14). Were there cryptocurrencies before Bitcoin? Investopedia. https://www.investopedia.com/tech/were-there-cryptocurrencies-Bitcoin/

Republic Compound LLC. (2021, July 31). Investing in Decentraland in 2021. Republic.co. https://republic.co/blog/real-estate/investing-in-decentraland-in-2021

River Financial. (n.d.). On-chain vs. off-chain Bitcoin transactions. River Financial. Retrieved July 24, 2021, from https://river.com/learn/on-chain-vs-off-chain-Bitcoin-transactions/

Robbins, J. (2021, April 25). Investors are buying land in virtual worlds. VOA. https://learningenglish.voanews.com/a/investors-are-buying-land-in-virtual-worlds-/5860444.html

Robertson, A. (2020, September 16). Facebook is discontinuing the Oculus Rift S. The Verge. https://www.theverge.com/2020/9/16/21422717/facebook-oculus-rift-s-discontinued-quest-2-vr-connect

Rossen, J. (2017, December 14). Before Bitcoin: The rise and fall of Flooz E-currency. Mentalfloss. https://www.mentalfloss.com/article/517911/Bitcoin-rise-and-fall-flooz-e-currency

Royalty, B. (2021, April 28). Music-focused NFTs from BAND Royalty allow fans to earn royalties from favorite songs. GlobeNewswire News Room. https://www.globenewswire.com/en/news-release/2021/04/28/2218770/0/en/Music-Focused-NFTs-from-BAND-Royalty-Allow-Fans-to-Earn-Royalties-from-Favorite-Songs.html

Shell. (n.d.). Blockchain. Retrieved July 16, 2021, https://www.shell.com/energy-and-innovation/digitalisation/digital-technologies/blockchain.html

Shelton, J. (2021, June 4). Non-fungible token honors a pioneering Yale statistician. YaleNews. https://news.yale.edu/2021/06/04/non-fungible-token-honors-pioneering-yale-statistician

Stassen, M. (2021, March 12). Music-related NFT sales have topped $25m in the past month. Music Business Worldwide. https://www.musicbusinessworldwide.com/music-related-nft-sales-have-topped-25m-in-the-past-month/

Steimle, E. (2019, October 25). Fractional ownership of art explained. Feral Blog. https://blog.feralhorses.co.uk/fractional-ownership-of-art-explained/

SuperRare. (n.d.). DESTINATION HEXAGONIA by Don Diablo. SuperRare. Retrieved July 20, 2021, https://superrare.com/artwork-v2/d%CE%BEstination-h%CE%BExagonia-by-don-diablo-23154

SuperRare. (2021, July 14). Product update: Personalized activity feed + new ways to discover. SuperRare. https://medium.com/superrare/product-update-personalized-activity-feed-new-ways-to-discover-ac9b606d42a8

Ten Hundred. (2021, March 9). My art almost destroyed the environment—The dark side of NFTs & cryptoArt [Video]. Youtube. https://www.youtube.com/watch?v=W7JVwbV2JBI

Thapa, S. (2021, July 8). 15 most expensive NFTs sold (so far). ScreenRant. https://screenrant.com/expensive-nfts-sold-so-far/

The Defiant. (2021, February 9). How to mint an NFT using Mintable [Video]. Youtube. https://www.youtube.com/watch?v=oZgobGr77NI

Vahia, S. (2021, July 10). Anthony Hopkins' new film will be sold as an NFT—Here's what that means for creators and the ones buying it. Business Insider. https://www.businessinsider.in/cryptocurrency/news/anthony-hopkins-new-film-will-be-sold-as-an-nft-heres-what-that-means-for-creators-and-the-ones-buying-it/articleshow/84289910.cms

Victor, M. (2021, March 27). Virtual worlds and NFTs—Decentraland & Co explained. Trust Wallet. https://trustwallet.com/blog/virtual-world-and-nfts-decentraland

Virtual reality. (2019, March 13). Wikipedia. https://en.wikipedia.org/wiki/Virtual_reality

[x]cube LABS. (2021, March 17). NFTs explained! Beginner's guide to non-fungible tokens. [X]Cube LABS. https://www.xcubelabs.com/blog/nfts-explained-beginners-guide-to-non-fungible-tokens/

Zucchi, K. (2020, June 30). Is Bitcoin mining still profitable? Investopedia. https://www.investopedia.com/articles/forex/051115/Bitcoin-mining-still-profitable.asp

All images were sourced from pixabay.com.

Made in the USA
Middletown, DE
01 December 2021

53933761R00066